Praise for *The Entre*

"This is one of the more engaging startup books I've read. It teaches principles of life as an entrepreneur in an enjoyable way that reaches the brain and heart simultaneously. The principles are core to startup success and are taught in a way that sticks."

—Carine S. Clark, founding member of Silicon Slopes and CEO

"*The Entrepreneur's Paradox* is the playbook for startup success. Grab this book and start winning."

—Sean Covey, president of FranklinCovey and coauthor of the #1 *Wall Street Journal* bestseller *The 4 Disciplines of Execution*

"The world needs entrepreneurs. And it needs the businesses these entrepreneurs create to flourish! Curtis Morley has done an outstanding job outlining the critical leadership and management requirements for all business leaders, especially those who have created and are running their own organizations. Filled with both tactical and strategic wisdom, this is a must-read!"

—Shawn D. Moon, *Wall Street Journal* bestselling author and CEO of Zerorez

"*The Entrepreneur's Paradox* is an essential book for taking your startup to the next level. Curtis Morley not only knows the path but has walked it many times."

—Dave Crenshaw, author of *The Myth of Multitasking*

"The principles taught in this book have been invaluable as I've been building my company, Acanela Expeditions. They have helped me personally develop the entrepreneurial skills needed to rise to the challenge of transforming myself into not only a successful entrepreneur, but also a successful leader. In this book you will read stories of climbing the tallest mountain in Africa, Mount Kilimanjaro. I was there with Curtis as we climbed Mount Kilimanjaro, and he has guided me as I have climbed the mountain of startup success. Building a successful company is similar in difficulty and also in reward. This is the guidebook on making it to the top of your own entrepreneurial mountain. You want to be a successful entrepreneur? Do it the smart and fast way and break free of the Paradox!"

—Kylie Chenn, founder and CEO of Acanella Expeditions

"Working with Curtis led to several quick epiphanies, brilliantly illuminating better and faster ways to create explosive growth. I doubled my business in one year's time using these principles and positioned my company perfectly for acquisition shortly thereafter."

—Scott Severe, CEO of ClientRunner Software

"They don't teach these principles in business school. These lessons can only come from the entrepreneurial book of life. Curtis has written the definitive playbook on how to win at the startup game."

—Kevin Cope, CEO and founder of Business Acumen and author of the #1 *New York Times* bestseller *Seeing the Big Picture*

"Curtis, I'm proud of you. You're bold, courageous even. You've written a powerful book that can, and will, change the life of anyone who reads it. Thank you for your abundant spirit that yearns to help others succeed. If you're a fellow traveler along the entrepreneurial path, this book is written for you.

"*The Entrepreneur's Paradox* is a reflection of Curtis's experiences run through the crucible of the real world. Read this book, apply the principles, and you'll find success in any business endeavor."

—Scott J. Miller, bestselling author of *Management Mess to Leadership Success* and Executive Vice President of Thought Leadership at FranklinCovey

"Curtis knows entrepreneurship. He openly shares his experiences and mistakes so you don't have to make them. This book is real! You won't be able to read it without exploring your soul and growing as an entrepreneur."

—David Horsager, CEO of the Trust Edge Leadership Institute and bestselling author

"Curtis Morley has the unique gift of translating life experience into actionable steps to success. *The Entrepreneur's Paradox* is a bold look into the principles and patterns behind scaling any startup. This book is an arrow aimed straight towards triumph."

—James Clarke, CEO and founder of Clarke Capital Partners

THE
ENTREPRENEUR'S
PARADOX

THE
ENTREPRENEUR'S
PARADOX

How to Overcome the 16 Pitfalls
Along the Startup Journey

BY CURTIS J MORLEY

FIU | Business Press
FLORIDA INTERNATIONAL UNIVERSITY
CORAL GABLES

Cover Design: Meridith Ethington
Cover Illustration: Meridith Ethington
Layout & Design: Roberto Núñez

For permission requests, please contact the publisher at:
Mango Publishing Group
2850 S Douglas Road, 2nd Floor
Coral Gables, FL 33134 USA
info@mango.bz

For special orders, quantity sales, course adoptions, and corporate sales, please email the publisher at sales@mango.bz. For trade and wholesale sales, please contact Ingram Publisher Services at customer.service@ingramcontent.com or +1.800.509.4887.

The Entrepreneur's Paradox: How to Overcome the 16 Pitfalls Along the Startup Journey

Library of Congress Cataloging-in-Publication number: 2020949837
ISBN: (print) 978-1-64250-412-5, (ebook) 978-1-64250-413-2
BISAC category code BUS025000, BUSINESS & ECONOMICS / Entrepreneurship

Printed in the United States of America

For Taylor, Austin, Brooke, Isaac, and Malia

I will love you forever.

Table of Contents

Pitfall 16

Introduction

Why This Book?

I sat in the upstairs dining area of the original Giordano's Deep Dish Pizzeria in Chicago, surrounded by signed pictures of celebrities, athletes, musicians, actors, politicians, and I'm fairly sure, a few local gangsters. The world-renowned pizza, smothered in fresh tomato sauce and layers of cheese, turned out to be nearly as deep as the conversation I was having with my friend, Greg. We were both entrepreneurs—me having started my first multimillion-dollar media agency at only twenty-six, and Greg having built a successful venture in Japan around the same time. My agency did everything from logo and branding design, radio and TV commercials, and trade shows, to heavy back-end database work. We specialized in interactive multimedia and rich internet application development. I even ranked second on an international certification for multimedia development. I loved being on the cutting edge of technology. I still do. It turned out for Greg and me that running our businesses was a part of our genetic makeup—the thought of not being some kind of entrepreneur just never occurred to either of us. If you've picked up this book because of the title, you likely know this feeling well.

Over the course of our dinner that evening, we wondered aloud, "Why doesn't everyone start their own business?"

For Greg, a guy whose monthly checks were bigger than most people's annual salaries, his entrepreneurial motivation was simple: "The reason I do my own thing is that I'm too lazy to do it the traditional way. I have to figure out a better and faster way to do business, so I don't have to work as hard as everyone else."

We both laughed heartily at the joke, but it held a golden nugget of truth: there is a better way to do business—to work smarter instead of harder. It is possible to start a company without the traditional years of headache and heartache.

And that's what this book is about: teaching you a better and faster way to create explosive growth in your business.

When Giordano's Pizza was founded in 1974, the Dow was at 580, and Warren Buffett was telling everyone, "This is the time to start investing." We didn't have the internet, so there wasn't the wealth of knowledge we have now about the principles required to start and grow a successful business. Without a relationship with someone like Warren Buffett, most startups stayed small or floundered. Take the story of Giordano's: two brothers, Efren and Joseph, took their mother's famous "Italian Easter Pie" recipe from Torino, Italy, to the US and opened their first restaurant. The pizza was so good they called the recipe a "sacred tradition," and I can attest it is one of the most savory pizzas I've ever eaten. The pizzeria received accolades from the *New York Times*, *Concierge Magazine*, CBS, NBC, and others. No question they had a recipe for an incredible pizza, but what about one for an incredible business? How many mistakes did they have to learn "the hard way"? How many sleepless nights did it take until they finally made it? If only their mother had left a "success tradition" recipe to follow as well.

Having a personal success recipe is a superb way to think about this book: a linear plan for building an amazing business and avoiding the painful and slow slog through the trenches, pitfalls, and numerous rookie mistakes. Had I been able to share this recipe with myself twenty years ago, I might have avoided several blunders launching and growing my first multimillion-dollar company. Viewed from the outside, I was winning awards, filing patents, working with most of the Fortune 500, expanding internationally, and being written up in magazines as one of the 40 under 40 entrepreneurs to watch. On the inside, however, I was nervous about how I would make the next payroll. I wouldn't wish that amount of stress and hand-wringing on anyone. And since I can't go back and mentor my younger self, I want to share my entrepreneurial recipe with you—a recipe grounded in principles and tested in the real world, that you can follow to accelerate revenue and profits.

There is a better way to do business today and you don't have to know Warren Buffett to take advantage of it. With the right mix of motivation, skill, and team members, it doesn't matter if you're crafting the world's best pizza or cooking up your own entrepreneurial dream.

And yet entrepreneurship is fraught with peril: 30 percent of all businesses in America fail in the first year and 50 percent fail in the first five. The truth is most businesses don't fail—entrepreneurs quit. The reason they quit is because the entrepreneurial process has sixteen pitfalls baked right in (pun intended). Each one of the pitfalls is an inflection point toward wild success or shutting the doors. Most entrepreneurs who have made it past the five-year mark have figured out how to navigate at least half a dozen pitfalls. The ones that make the news because of rapid growth fly past these pitfalls masterfully. That's what this book is about.

Like Mama Giordano's "Sacred Tradition," the recipe for navigating past these pitfalls didn't come from the halls of an elite culinary school (a.k.a. an MBA) but the hard-won experience of trial and error in the real world (mixed with a few years leading the global marketing effort for one of the world's premier leadership companies). And yet nearly all entrepreneurs (including myself) contend with these pitfalls every time they set out to build a new business.

In my case, I remember thinking *my* business was special…that I was creating something that had never been done before. It was easy to take that belief and assume it would be enough to fuel the momentum to succeed. Destiny, here I come!

But it wasn't so easy, despite my business truly being one of a kind and with a *modus operandi* that was even more unique. Very few companies around the world were creating interactive media the way we were, and the creators of the software we used said they'd never seen a more advanced Rich Internet Application (RIA). So, with a new patent and industry awards under our belt, it makes sense that it would all have fallen together perfectly. Only it didn't, and I wasn't prepared for the price I had to pay to make it all happen.

Later, as I reflected on this experience and the experiences I was seeing as a consultant, I could see a pattern at work: my start-up clients were experiencing the same pains I had pushed through years before. For example, they would typically hit an invisible ceiling within the first couple of years. They were experiencing the same personnel issues within the first few years. My clients were trying to find the path to rapid growth in the same way I had experienced it. They found similar challenges at each financial milestone (such as five, ten, and twenty million in revenue), as well as other inflection points that I had experienced—and often in the same order.

If you feel that pull toward starting your own business and are ready to jump into the start-up waters (or, having already jumped in, you're feeling you may be in over your head), I've written this book for you as a:

- Visionary looking to take your idea, product, or service and turn it into a viable business

- Business owner looking for rapid growth and revenue

- Founder of a start-up looking not only to survive but thrive in the days to come

The Paradox

"No is the amplifier of Yes."

—CRAWFORD CRAGUN

> "Entrepreneur's Paradox: You have to give up being the best in the world at building your product to be the best in the world at building your business."

At the core of this book is a paradox: what got you into business is the very thing that will actively prevent you from succeeding in business.

That's right—you, the entrepreneur, are typically one of the most proficient people in the world at a particular skill, craft, product, or idea. You've thought of or created something that has never been done before, especially in the way you've conceived it. When others find out about how great your idea is, they ask for, even demand, your product or service. In fact, they often love the product or service so much they compel you to start a business repeating that expertise over and over again. It can be thrilling knowing you can contribute to the world and seeing how many people appreciate what you do and the way you do it. But such a passion can create its own kind of trap. In the beginning, everything feels exciting and the business appears to be thriving (if it weren't for this honeymoon phase, I'm not sure anyone would start a business). But that newfound freedom can quickly shackle you with grueling hours and endless to-do lists. And where you thought you would find personal and financial independence, there's stress, erratic cash flow, and bills instead.

This book will show you how that initial spark of brilliance and entrepreneurial spirit can be the very thing that inhibits entrepreneurs from achieving their goals—regardless of industry or business type. But by recognizing and working through the chapters in this book, you can learn to work through the Entrepreneur's Paradox and experience growth equal to the passion that gave it life.

Who This Book Is For (And Not For)

This is not a management technique book. I have not aimed it at large corporations or start-up founders who have already had multiple equity events or an IPO. Although many in the corporate world will find this book helpful, I've written it for those in the entrepreneurial trenches. I wrote this book for start-up entrepreneurs looking for a way to create rapid growth and break through to the next level. It is for founders of companies typically in the first two to ten years of business. And it is for first-time entrepreneurs needing a tool to avoid many of the missteps that doom new ventures. As a result, after reading this book, you will walk away with:

- Proven ideas for your company to achieve rapid growth

- Life-changing directions to follow as a new entrepreneur

- Awareness of how you can either inhibit or energize your business goals

- A clear path to navigate past the pitfalls standing between you and success

You'll also find this book includes links to many online resources, calculators, infographics, and tools for the "Overcoming the Pitfalls" sections at the end of each chapter to help you self-assess and move your business forward. Some principles relate to the business, and many relate directly to you as the entrepreneur. And by the way, if you're reading this well above your mid-twenties and think it may be too late to start your entrepreneurial journey, take heart. According to the Wharton Knowledge Group, you'll enjoy some advantages that come with age and experience.[1] It's both never too early and never too late to answer the call and take this journey.

So, get ready to dig in and go deep as an entrepreneur—not unlike digging in and going deep with that Chicago pizza. Because it's one thing to have a world-class offering, and quite another to build the world-class business around it. Pull up a chair, take a seat at the table, grab a slice, and let's get to it.

1   Nov 12, 2. (n.d.). The Average Age of Successful Entrepreneurs Is Actually 45. Retrieved September 14, 2020, from knowledge.wharton.upenn.edu/article/age-of-successful-entrepreneurs.

The Entrepreneur's Paradox

"Man conquers the world by conquering himself."

— ZENO OF CITIUM

I awoke at four thirty with the grid pattern of my keyboard imprinted on the side of my face. Sleep-deprived and groggy, I was the only one left in the office. The keyboard had become my unintentional pillow repeatedly for nearly three days, and I found myself in a kind of bleary-eyed delirium. I wanted to sleep, but there was too much work to do.

I'd started my new company to find freedom, wealth, and excitement, but instead I found myself in a prison of my own making. My entrepreneurial dream had been marked by insane work hours, sleepless nights, no after-hours teammates, grueling deadlines, and difficult clients. I often wished I had more time for my family, church callings, writing and playing music, and pushing harder on triathlons.

I'd traded a really great boss at Ancestry.com for a crack-the-whip, ruthless tyrant: me! I'd also exchanged normal work hours, stable cash flow, and time with my family for marathon work sessions away from home, crazy amounts of stress, and erratic cash flow. This prison of my own making—my personal gilded cage—held a single sign over the barred door which read, "Entrepreneurship."

I pushed through that morning to finish the project on time, staying focused on the usual high quality it demanded.

From the outside, my business looked like it was succeeding. I'd received the "Entrepreneur of the Year" award from the Chamber of Commerce and was listed as one of the "40 under 40" taking advantage of the fast-growing economy in the Silicon Slopes (a technology hub at the base of the Wasatch Mountains in Utah). I had been written up in magazines like *Utah Business* and *Business Q* and was recognized as one of the leading interactive website and multimedia developers in the world. A professional international certification ranked me second in the world in Adobe Flash. All the trappings of success, right? Turns out, not so much.

How did I get here?

I didn't have the answer that morning, and it took several years and more than one painful lesson (including losing my first company to a corporate coup) to help me see how I'd trapped myself despite all my talents, passions, and work ethic. Once I'd lost the company, I pushed the reset button and reevaluated my world view. I changed my paradigms and took a hard look at my professional life from a more objective point of view.

That's when the epiphany came. I'd been caught in a paradox—the Entrepreneur's Paradox, to be more precise. In short, I was good at what I did—*really* good. But this was the reason my business wasn't succeeding.

Think about it for a moment. If you're highly skilled at something, people view you as an expert and want your hands-on efforts. Clients see *you* and not *the business* as the most expedient path to that "magic" you sold them in the first place. My clients were no different. They wanted *me, Curtis*. They weren't really interested in the services of *my business*. I had employees, tools, and a few systems in place, but our corporate clients wanted me, personally, to do the work. After all, I had been the one doing the work for other clients in the past. As a young and inexperienced entrepreneur, I had made the mistake of assuming that "doing the work" and "growing the business" were the same thing. But they are as different as night and day.

With this new (and hard-won) insight, I realized that, if I wanted to succeed in business, I had to stop being the sole expert, the sought-after specialist, the best in the world. I had to give up part of my identity.

The Entrepreneur's Paradox applies not only to me, but also to countless others who attempt the leap from world-class expert and specialist to business owner. You simply can't be the best in the world at your craft while being best in the world at running a business. As the saying goes, "No man can serve two masters." And that's exactly what I, and most entrepreneurs, have tried to do.

Our personal passions are often at the heart of a new business venture. One of my friends is a chocolatier because of his love for chocolate. Another started a travel expedition company because she loves to travel and has a true talent for immersing people in unique cultural experiences. Another friend started a video game company because of his love and talent for gaming. Still another started a mobile app company because he has a passion for clean design and journaling and wanted to help people around the world tell their stories. Passion is great fodder for the entrepreneurial engine.

In the years between that first business epiphany and the writing of this book, I've coached many passionate entrepreneurs. Without fail, they all talk about how unique their business is—that they have the secret sauce that will differentiate and propel them past their competitors. And it's often true. But what tends to *always* be true is the timeline these entrepreneurs will go through. Their stories are almost always the same and move in predictable chapters and verses.

Entrepreneur's Island

All entrepreneurs start somewhere else in life. They usually start at an established company. Most get a little taste of entrepreneurship when they take a small break from the "normal" world. Instead of waking up each day to go to the same office and see the same boss and do the same thing day in and day out, they get a taste of something new and exciting, tapping into their skills and being rewarded emotionally and monetarily. It's like taking a vacation to a tropical island where breaking waves offer adventure and pristine white sand beaches and which seems like a little piece of heaven. It's exhilarating because it represents many of the things we enjoy and are passionate about. It comes with a rush of new experiences and we are often praised for our accomplishments there, because we are typically very skilled at what we do. Most will occasionally jump to the island for a fleeting moment of thrilling experiences and then bounce back from this "special" world to the ordinary, safe, and comfortable world (i.e., our day jobs). In today's vernacular, this is often called freelancing, moonlighting, or even having a "side hustle." Yet, we still feel the pull of this island and can't wait to go back.

For others, this desire becomes so strong we leave the comfort of the ordinary world permanently—selling our homes on the mainland and moving to the island! At first, it's a paradise. We wake up whenever it feels nice, set our schedule according to what suits us best, and have fun doing what we love. This is the life! And people really appreciate the artistry with which we build our sandcastles, fish for food, and make the most delicious coconut drinks (i.e., the products or services we offer). Even better, the demand for our products grows.

Then, one day, as we are sitting on our beach chair, we hear a rustle in the vegetation from behind. We turn to catch sight of an alligator creeping out of the jungle and heading straight for us! The alligator threatens our livelihood, peace, and food. Springing into action, we're forced to wrestle it away from our beautiful beach and the delicious fish cooking over the fire. Not only will this beast crush our castles in the sand, but it will deprive us of food and all we've accomplished. The alligators show up in the form of unrealistic deadlines, unplanned emergencies, keeping customers happy, cash flow issues, and a host of other activities that require our time, energy, and focus. We didn't realize life on Entrepreneur's Island came with a cost! When we saw the shimmering blue ocean waves, we had no idea there were alligators native to our little patch of paradise.

Over time, more alligators begin to show up. It seems the longer we live on the island and the bigger the fish we reel in, the more alligators we attract. Long gone is the fantasy of sipping drinks from coconuts and basking under the ocean sun. Instead, each day brings a new assault and a greater struggle to wrestle these alligators away. The cost of maintaining life in paradise is to spend a greater portion of each day wrestling these unwelcome intruders. And to make matters worse, it seems that when one gets a bite, it attracts even more!

Fed up and tired of being surprised day in and day out, we decide to find the home of these alligators and deal with the problem head-on. That means leaving the beach and entering the jungle. If it can keep our beach safe, it's worth the effort. Trudging through the dense brush, we find the swamp the alligators call home. There's little choice but to jump in and start wrestling, and this is how we spend the majority of the day: resolving client concerns, answering emails, returning phone calls, reconciling bank accounts, filing taxes, finishing projects, fixing projects, looking for new projects, scheduling travel, building a website, invoicing…the list of alligators is nearly endless. But we wrestle them one by one, even though it means returning to the beach later and later each day. What's strange is that we actually become quite good at wrestling alligators and keeping them off the beach, even though it's a beach we see less and less of.

This isn't where we wanted to be when we left the comfort of a stable job. We wanted to be in a place of freedom, flexibility, wealth, praise, and excitement. Well, we got the excitement for sure. We've entered our personal version of *Groundhog Day*: wake up, wrestle alligators, go to bed, repeat. It's exhausting and doesn't feel like that magical island we sacrificed everything to move to.

Draining the Swamp

> "Alligators: The urgent demands and important tasks incumbent to running your business and which can't be ignored."

Entrepreneur's Island is made up of an idyllic beach where you *wanted* to spend your time, a thick jungle with a swamp full of alligators you were *forced* to wrestle, and several tall mountains in the distance you *hardly noticed* (if at all). So after months (or years) of wrestling alligators, it's time to make a choice: swap your title from "entrepreneur" to "alligator wrestler" and learn to accept the reality of your work life, or find a smaller section of beach, less inviting to alligators, where you can downsize and go back to a simple (smaller) life. Or reject both those options and choose a third alternative. For me, this is when the words of my friend Greg started resonating in my head: *There is a better way. Stop wrestling alligators.*

If you want to stop wrestling the alligators, you must "drain the swamp." Because, once you drain the swamp, the alligators will leave on their own. But it isn't easy. As the saying goes, "It's hard to drain the swamp when you're always eye-to-eye with an alligator."

So, how do you break free and escape? First, you have to recognize the *why* behind your alligator wrestling. And it begins with the fact that *you* are the expert and that becomes your identity. I've seen entrepreneurs hold tightly to being the magazine *editor* rather than the magazine *owner*, the brilliant *programmer* rather than the brilliant *business person,* the game-changing *engineer* rather than *engineering* an incredible company. Most entrepreneurs hold tightly to the identity of being the best in the world at building a product or offering a service, rather than being the best in the world at building a company. But being the expert means you have to be the person performing the tasks every day. People love you for it, and you love the feeling of creating something amazing. But in reality, this is diving into the swamp.

Because you're the expert and actively engaged in alligator wrestling, you're essentially doing everything by yourself. Trust me, I get it. I know the feeling of producing something that has never been done before. I know how fulfilling it is to produce something beautiful, creative, and exceptional. The trouble is, as long as you are the one producing the product or service, you have no time to drain the swamp. The way out is to create systems and processes, including training others to create the product or deliver the service as well as you do, so you can create a business equally as amazing as your product. More on that in future chapters.

The paradox is that these talents and skills were what brought you to the beach in the first place. These are the things that served you in creating your company but now are holding you back and keeping you stuck. These are the things you have to let go of in order to be able to take a step back and figure out how to drain the swamp.

A New Identity

Marshall Goldsmith coined the phrase, "What got you here won't get you there." In entrepreneurship, what got you here will actively prevent you from getting there. It will be so dominating in your life that you won't even be able to see that there is a whole new world of possibilities beyond the swamp. It's time to redirect your passion for the product or service you create and focus it toward building a sustainable business free from nightly keyboard imprints on your face.

Part of changing your identity is acknowledging that you are **not** your business. Although your business is a living, breathing organism, and has a life of its own, many entrepreneurs will take the identity of the business upon themselves. Here's an easy survey to assess whether you've assumed your business's identity:

- Did you name the company after yourself?

- Do your bank account and the company bank account share the same number?

- When your business is doing well, do you feel like *you* are succeeding?

- Is your business defining you?

- Does every success feel like it is your personal success?

- Does every business failure feel fatal to you, personally?

You are not defined by your business, and the healthiest and fastest way to grow your company is to disassociate your identity from the identity of the business. You are a piece of your company. Arguably the most important piece, but still just a piece. If the business were a person, you'd be the heart and often the brains of the company, but you are not *the* company. Be willing to let the business have its own identity independent of you. Set up a separate bank account. Think about rebranding your company with a catchy descriptive name that is not your own. Surrender the fact that your company can and needs to thrive without your direct labor. With this mindset, you will grow faster, be healthier, and see the results you are looking for.

You must let go of these two parts of your old identity (I am the best in the world at my craft, and me and my business are the same) and take on a new one. I am independent of my company and not afraid to let others take over tasks that are meaningful and important; I am the business builder and no longer the product builder. Instead of you being the most skilled at travel, interactive technologies, programming, guitar building, video games, or whatever you identify with, you'll need to stop the full-time job of fighting alligators and focus all of your attention on being the **business builder**—the one who drains the swamp. This means you will need to:

- **Build a team**. Hire a full-time assistant and other skilled individuals you can offload tasks to. Look into hiring or recruiting interns as well, as many universities provide a mechanism to trade work experience for credit. Many of them

can transition to employees as they graduate, and you'll already
have a positive and effective working relationship.

- **Delegate responsibilities**. Use full-time, contract, and on-call
  professionals (such as an accountant and lawyer) to engage in
  their areas of expertise.

- **Implement software and systems**. Equip tools, systems, and
  processes so critical parts of the business can run efficiently
  and without your constant attention.

- **Train your team**. You'll need to bridge the gap as the "expert"
  and help instruct, coach, and mentor your staff to deliver high-
  quality products and services and deliver premier customer
  service just as you would.

Taking actions like those listed above will help you shift from service
provider and/or product builder to that of *company* builder. Your
charge is to get out of the day-to-day. **Make a commitment today to
start draining the swamp and never return.**

Remember, draining the swamp is a *process*. It will take time figuring
out how to make sure the secret sauce you bring to the business is
disseminated to others. Spend your days focused on the bigger picture
rather than focusing myopically on the creation of the product or
service. For me, in my first company, this meant I needed to stop
being the best in the world at building interactive media. I had to
abandon that persona and the praise and excitement that went with
it. This kind of identity shift is a difficult task. It's not familiar or
comfortable, especially at first. I understand. Yet it's critical if you
are going to take your business to the next level. Because once you're
past the swamp, there are mountains to climb. Remember those
mountains on Entrepreneur's Island you hardly took notice of?
That's where we're headed next. So come along, we've got quite the
journey ahead!

The Entrepreneur's Paradox: Apply the Principle

- Reinvent yourself as an entrepreneur and not just a skilled specialist or artisan. Stop building the product and start building the business.

- Write down the reasons your product is successful, capturing the recipe you've used to make it successful, for example:

  - I pay attention to detail in my work.

  - I think outside the box when creating my product.

  - I'm passionate about what I produce.

  - I know what my customers want in the product.

- Write out how these principles can apply to your business as a whole.

- Take one of your full workdays and track all the activities you engage in. Write down everything you do and how much time you spend on each. Mark the FEEDING THE ALLIGATORS column for any activity that doesn't lead to the strategic enhancement of the company and mark the DRAINING THE SWAMP column for any activity that boosts your business strategy.

- With your list of weekly activities in front of you, start creating a permanent "To Don't" list. Identify at least ten things you will stop doing or will delegate to others so you can free up your time to focus on creating a better business.

  - NOTE: If you are part-time freelancing, moonlighting, or running a "side hustle," you may not have the resources to hire everybody on the list. If you're making over 10K a year, spend a few hundred dollars and hire an accountant. Then scale from there.

Activity	Time Spent	Wrestling Alligators	Draining the Swamp
Sorting mail	15 minutes	x	
Working on my five-year business plan	1 hour, 10 minutes		x
Arranging travel for upcoming client visit	50 minutes	x	
Create onboarding process for new employees	2 hours		x
Payroll	1 hour 35 minutes	x	
Finishing the logo for a new client	2 hours 20 minutes	x	
Create an org chart of positions needed to take the company to the next level	1 hour 30 minutes		x
Bookkeeping and filing quarterly taxes	1 hour 35 minutes	x	
Meeting with client and revising graphics for website	2 hours, 50 minutes	x	
Formatting spreadsheet to make it look more presentable	35 minutes	x	
Meeting with a mentor or coach for lunch	2 hours		x
Identifying a plan to overcome the top three stumbling blocks	2 hours 10 minutes		x

A printable activity tracker can be found on the web at
EntrepreneursParadox.com/ActivityTracker

Pitfall 1

Seeing the Swamp and Not the Mountains

"If you don't know where you are going, any road will get you there."

—LEWIS CARROLL, AUTHOR OF *ALICE'S ADVENTURES IN WONDERLAND*

I love seeing when the entrepreneurs I work with have the "light bulb moment." This moment happens when, maybe for the first time, they begin to see past the swamp to the mountain range waiting to take them to new heights. Entrepreneur's Island has always had mountains, but the monotonous and tiring daily drudge of wrestling alligators distracts entrepreneurs and keeps their attention focused on the swamp. Every start-up has a swamp full of alligators and every start-up has majestic mountains to conquer. The sad truth is that most entrepreneurs never make it past the swamp to begin their ascent. For the lucky ones who find the mountains on the island, they are able to take a completely different journey full of adventure. In the real world as I've worked with clients, I've heard this realization expressed countless times in more or less the same way: "I didn't really think about what my company could eventually become because I've been so heads down this whole time."

This is the first light bulb moment, when the entrepreneur sees the mountain and realizes that, if they are willing to completely change their identity and remove themselves from the swamp, they can achieve great things. The second big aha is when they realize their entire reality just shattered and now they have no idea where to start! But like my clients, if you're willing to break free from the paradox and change your identity from service provider/product builder to business builder, you're ready to chart a course forward while avoiding the common pitfalls along the way. Pitfall 1 is about seeing past the swamp and jungle thicket and discovering the exciting mountains waiting for you to climb.

Begin with the End in Mind by Picking Your Mountain Range

"One day Alice came to a fork in the road and saw a Cheshire cat in a tree.
'Which road do I take?' she asked.
'Where do you want to go?' was his response.
'I don't know,' Alice answered.
'Then,' said the cat, 'it doesn't matter.'"

> "Beginning with the End in Mind means to begin each day, task, or project with a clear vision of your desired direction and destination, and then continue by flexing your proactive muscles to make things happen."[2]

When forming a start-up, most entrepreneurs don't "begin with the end in mind" as the late Dr. Stephen R. Covey said. Instead, they start with the beginning in mind. What I mean by this is that most entrepreneurs want to create something cool, that has never been done before, and will change the world. But then what? What's the next step *after* you create the next Facebook or TikTok? What do you do with your product or service after you create the idea?

Consider the history of the electric car. If I were to ask you the year, make, and inventor of the first electric car, what would you say? Elon Musk and the Tesla Roadster he released in 2008? How about Nissan and their electric Leaf? As it turns out, it was neither. The first production electric car was built in 1884 by Thomas Parker, a British inventor. Never heard of him? Don't worry, no one ever has. Simply creating something revolutionary is not enough. Parker's invention was groundbreaking and could have dramatically changed the world and the environment, if he had had the vision to go beyond the invention. Many people confuse being an inventor (or even an innovator) with being an entrepreneur. I certainly did in my first business. I thought if I built the most amazing, award-winning websites and interactive multimedia, the most revolutionary rich internet applications, or the best apps known to mankind, that would be enough. But being an inventor/innovator is not the same as being an entrepreneur. The paradox of focusing on the product and not the company kept me struggling in the swamp and wrestling alligators.

---

2   Habit 2: Begin with End in Mind. (n.d.). Retrieved September 07, 2020, from www.franklincovey.com/the-7-habits/habit-2.html.

The Speed of Business

"S&P 500: The Standard & Poor's 500 (S&P 500) Index is a grouping of the 500 largest US publicly traded companies. The index includes many high-tech and financial businesses."

"IPO: Initial Public Offering (IPO), is the procedure a privately held company uses to 'Go Public' or start selling stock on the stock market or other exchange to outside investors. This highly regulated process is used to raise capital by selling shares of the company to the public. It is governed by the Securities and Exchange Commission (SEC)."

In the past, startups had the luxury to grow for decades in isolated markets, and the global economy was more of an idea than an actuality. The model had been built by names like Rockefeller and Buffett, and it required a mentor steeped in expertise to teach the secrets of building a successful company. But today the speed of business is accelerating at a rapid pace. For example, in 1935 the average lifespan of a company on the S&P 500 was ninety years. In 2020, the average lifespan of a company on the S&P 500 is only eighteen years. And it's predicted that, by 2027, that number will drop to only twelve years and 75 percent of companies on the list in 2012 will be gone by 2027!

YEARS, ROLLING 7 YEAR AVERAGE
Average Company Lifespan on S&P 500 Index

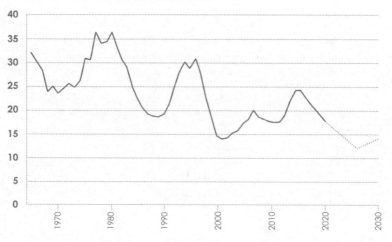

Data: Analysis based on public S&P 500 data sources.

This trend raises the question: why is the lifespan of companies on
the S&P 500 decreasing? Why are they disappearing so quickly?
It's because the speed of business is increasing. Companies are able
to reach profitability faster, capture market share sooner, and hit
their stride earlier. Because of all this, they are becoming acquisition
targets more speedily. All of these factors also mean the largest
companies can be overtaken by new startups in ways that were never
thought possible in the past. Startups are going public in fewer years
and technology is advancing at an astonishing pace. Systems have
been created that accelerate sales, marketing, customer relationship
management, and finances, spinning the business life cycle faster and
faster. You no longer have to be an apprentice to the titans of industry
to become the next big thing. You just need to tap into the principles
of entrepreneurship that have already been discovered and avoid the
most common pitfalls.

The Three Mountain Ranges

To begin with the end in mind means deciding *what kind* of business you want to run. This comes down to a choice between the three mountain ranges found on Entrepreneur's Island:

- **The Lifestyle Range**. Adorned by the smallest and most navigable mountains, this range is marked by small, typically one-shop businesses focused on earning enough cash to support a desired company culture and/or lifestyle. But there are plenty of pitfalls for the unwary: it looks deceptively easy (but it's not). One of the greatest risks is a loss of passion.

   - Real-world example: *The Wasatch Range; Mt. Timpanogos.*

- **The Buy or Be Bought Range**. Marked by significantly higher mountains with more technical paths to the summit, this range consists of entrepreneurs building businesses in preparation of an acquisition or a merger with another company. For many, the mountains found on the Buy or Be Bought Range represent the most compelling reward for the time and effort required to get to the top. Mountains found on this range can be exciting to tackle, as things take off quickly and it's likely others around you will take note. Recognition and awards may come quickly, but climbing a mountain on this range requires a greater degree of preparation, team support, and leadership prowess.

   - Real-world example: *The Eastern Rift Mountains; Mt. Kilimanjaro*

- **The IPO / Private Offering Range**. Home of the very highest and most technically demanding Public Offering mountains. This range is impossible to navigate without highly trained experts, careful planning and preparation, and a willingness to follow a very exacting route that allows little or no error. This is not a range for novices to attempt. It is fraught with pitfalls at practically every step. Making the final ascent to the summit, however, can be truly life changing.

   - Real-world example: *The Himalayas; Mt. Everest.*

The need to start with the end in mind and determine where you want to take your business is essential to success—you simply cannot wait. So let's take a closer look at the three types of businesses in more detail:

THE LIFESTYLE BUSINESS

A lifestyle business is what you typically think of as the flower shop on the corner, the piano teacher, the blogger with wanderlust, or the local fruit stand—a typical "mom and pop" establishment or a freewheeling hipster traveling throughout the world. It's about work/life balance without a pressing need to grow dramatically, grab market dominance, or have an incredible Initial Public Offering (IPO). Lifestyle businesses are not trying to get bought; they're just doing what they do day in and day out and produce revenue. That doesn't mean they have to be small, either. I know several multimillion-dollar lifestyle companies that go out of their way to build a culture that's bigger than just what happens at the office.

It's important to note that, while lifestyle businesses can succeed, of the three options, they are the hardest to sustain long-term. In today's business climate, if a company's not adequately growing, it's slowly dying. For example, consider a lifestyle start-up that in year one, given their small niche, managed to earn $200,000 in revenue. Then, in year two, they realized $215,000, on track for $235,000 in year three (and so on). Although the numbers look positive, that won't tell the entire story. The market growth might be 20 percent in their industry, so growing at less than 10 percent per year actually means they are losing market share. One of the risks in a lifestyle business is that, given today's speed of business, a competitor could be eating up the market share. Or, market forces could have changed so rapidly, the product or service may be on its way to irrelevance—despite steady increases in top-line revenue.

In my experience, lifestyle businesses are the most difficult of the three. This isn't to say a lifestyle business isn't a viable option. In fact, if your focus is having more time or flexibility, and you love the satisfaction of the creative process, this can be a great goal. History suggests this is not the ideal route for producing extreme wealth, but some companies do achieve great results. One such company I'm familiar with is called TestOut. This is a company that does certification training for popular IT and computer technologies and has been able to attain and maintain a profitable business that provides a great lifestyle for the owner and employees. In fact, they are profitable enough that they have provided a yearly cruise for every employee and their significant other as a year-end bonus. You can imagine the expense of doing this. The founder, Noel Vallejo, has learned to navigate the mountain and avoid the pitfalls as outlined in this book.

In my home state is a majestic mountain called Mount Timpanogos, my real-world equivalent to a Lifestyle Mountain on Entrepreneur's Island. The mountain is named after a beautiful American Indian princess, and if you look closely, the ridge of the mountain outlines the resting maiden's form. This peak rises from the valley floor to a height of 11,752 feet. To get to the top of the mountain, you hike along a well-worn trail traveled by many others, which is beautifully adorned with wildflowers. It's common to see herds of mountain goats, bighorn sheep, and maybe even an elk or moose. The hike begins just above the famous Sundance ski resort and is seven and a half miles one-way (fifteen round trip) with an elevation gain of 4,580 feet. Many will embark in the early twilight hours to reach the summit in time for the sunrise. The hike is not easy, but it's also not hard. Children make the trip as well as eighty-year-olds. In order to make it up, one requires a good set of lungs, a couple liters of water, a nice peanut butter and jelly sandwich (or two), and enough time to get up and back. People do this hike in nice hiking sandals and shorts, and some people even run the entire trail! If that sounds like the metaphorical equivalent to the kind of mountains you want to climb as an entrepreneur, the lifestyle business model may be the one for you.

THE BUY OR BE BOUGHT BUSINESS

Most entrepreneurs dream about this end. In today's economy, many companies are seeing successful exits through acquisition. Some haven't even reached profitability, yet they're still being acquired by either investment firms, private equity, strategic buyers, or competitors. One advantage of the "Buy or Be Bought" strategy is that in order to buy other companies, a start-up either has enough profit to fund the acquisition themselves or they have an investor who believes in their business model and execution enough to give them cash to purchase other companies. My most recent company, eLearning Brothers, was one of these companies, and has purchased eight other companies in the last six years. At first, the acquisitions were small. But as the company grew, the acquisitions grew and became more strategic. If the two original brothers who founded eLearning Brothers hadn't decided on a buy or be bought mountain climb, such acquisitions would have never happened.

The real-world equivalent to the Buy or Be Bought Mountains is Mt. Kilimanjaro, the largest freestanding mountain in the world. It towers over the African continent at 19,341 feet and is a behemoth not to be taken lightly. It requires both physical training and altitude training before embarking on the expedition. Climbing is a multi-day trip, and the governments of Tanzania and Zimbabwe require guides and porters be hired to lead adventurers along the way. Much like Timpanogos, the climb can be started in shorts, with an average temperature of around eighty-four at the base of the mountain. But at the top it can drop to a frigid negative twenty degrees! There are five different climate zones on the mountain and multiple sets of clothes and gear are required. *Base camp* for this mountain is 3,678 feet above the peak of Timpanogos, and the climb takes much more food than a few peanut butter and jelly sandwiches and a protein bar. The necessity for water is such that no CamelBak will hold enough, and it must be collected and filtered along the route. Hypoxia (altitude sickness) is just one of several life-threatening risks involved with making the climb. But once you summit, the views from the top are breathtaking. If that sounds like the metaphorical equivalent to the kind of mountains you want to climb as an entrepreneur, the buy or be bought model may be the one for you.

THE IPO BUSINESS

"Private Equity: Private equity is an investment vehicle to get funding. Private equity can come from funds, investment groups and direct private investors often called Angel Investors."

"Unicorn: A privately held start-up with a valuation higher than one billion dollars."

The last option is to create a company that does an initial public (or private) offering. An IPO is a large and public way for a start-up founder to receive a significant payday. Unfortunately, most entrepreneurs don't see the company from the start to an IPO as they need to hit specific revenue numbers, require a private equity group backing them, and fail to overcome the other complexities, investments, regulations, and legalities necessary to succeed. But there are some amazing entrepreneurs, like Aaron Skonnard of the unicorn company, Pluralsight, a video training company, who stuck with the company from inception to investment to IPO. Pluralsight was founded by three partners who literally climbed a mountain in the Himalayan range and read books on investment strategies. The Pluralsight IPO raised $310.5 million and priced 20.7 million shares at fifteen dollars per share. With more than 14,000 business customers, 695,000 end-users, and 6,700 on-demand online courses, they are an example of an IPO success. Even though the company valuation is now over four billion dollars, they started out like most entrepreneurs, with a dream and desire to make it work.

Our real-world equivalent to this Entrepreneur's Island mountain range would have to be Mt. Everest itself. Rising 29,029 feet into the clouds, Base Camp-1 is nearly as high as the summit of Kilimanjaro! The summit requires multiple trips up and down to various camps to acclimatize to the altitude and can push even experienced climbers emotionally and physically. This is the mountain of all mountains, and includes a technical climb using ladders to span crevasses in the ice at the Khumbu Icefall, as well other specialized equipment. Many who have attempted the climb have not made it back. It's long, it's far, it's hard, it's expensive, and it's the penultimate adventure. Oxygen is expected in the Death Zone above 26,000 feet and sherpas are not optional; they are required to make it back alive. If that sounds like the metaphorical equivalent to the kind of mountains you want to climb as an entrepreneur (and you acknowledge you're not a novice and can navigate the various perils of such a climb), then the IPO model may be the one for you.

Pick Your Destination: What Is Your "End in Mind"?

Regardless of which mountain range you choose, each will provide an incredible adventure with amazing rewards. In addition, each range will require a very different set of actions, supplies, training, and help as you ultimately pick *your* individual mountain within that range and begin the climb to the summit. The key at this point is to pick one, because once you know where you want to go, you will start to naturally align your time and energy toward it. And because of such a focus, once you put it out into the universe, it's almost as if the universe conspires to make it come true. Consult the chart below as a final review as you weigh your options and decide which mountain range (business type) you will chart a course toward:

	Lifestyle Business	Buy or Be Bought (Merger and Acquisition)	IPO
Focus	Profitability	Rapid Growth	Beating financial projections
Acceptable Growth Rates	Any amount of growth	Rapid Growth is paramount	Beat current market growth
Corporate Structure	Sole proprietorship, partnership, S-Corp	LLC or S-Corp	C-Corp
Revenue	Typically smaller dollars, from a few hundred thousand to a couple million	Increasing revenue in the mid to high eight to nine figure range	Hundreds of millions to billions in revenue
Profitability	Key Focus over growth: lifestyle companies done right can spin off much profit	Not the primary concern if revenue and customer growth is high	Balanced with growth
Lifestyle	Extremely flexible and unfettered	High demand yet flexible	High demand and market pressure
Market share	Not a concern	Grab market share as fast as possible sometimes at the expense of profit	Focused effort to capture market share but not at the expense of profitability
Revenue per employee	Enough to cover costs and have a small return	Flexible number based on growth and hiring patterns	One of the key metrics for evaluating company health

	Lifestyle Business	Buy or Be Bought (Merger and Acquisition)	IPO
Headcount	Few to no employees	Several hundred to thousands	Thousands to tens of thousands
Financing	Loans, Internal financing, friends and family	Venture capital, debt financing	Private equity and stock market
Regulations	Minimal regulations	Minimal regulations	Highly regulated

Overcoming Pitfall 1: Move Past the Swamp and Pick Your Mountain

- Pick a mountain. Decide whether you want to run a lifestyle business, have an acquisition strategy, or work toward an IPO.

- If you are having trouble deciding, go to the website and take the survey to guide you through: EntrepreneursParadox.com/MountainSurvey.

- Read more case studies on the different business types. EntrepreneursParadox.com/CaseStudies.

- Based on which path you choose, research the story of three to five companies that took a similar path. If there are local companies that have climbed similar mountains in your area, invite the founder to lunch. If the founder is different from the current CEO, schedule a lunch with the CEO as well and ask them to share their experience.

Pitfall 2

Climbing Without a Map

A fate much worse than blindness is having sight without the vision to see.

In the last chapter, we identified three potential mountain ranges worthy of your climbing endeavors: the Lifestyle Range, the Buy or Be Bought Range, and the IPO Range. Each has its own challenges and requires different equipment, routes, and strategies to make it to the top. And within each of these ranges, there is a mountain specifically your own. It is a specific peak made just for you. Now that you know that you can climb to new heights, it's time to pick the peak by creating a plan that is more than just a hope, dream, or vision.

You've moved past the swamp and the exhausting task of alligator wrestling, you take a deep breath and turn your gaze upward; there, in the distance, are the majestic and inspiring peaks awaiting your ascent. They are your dreams; your yet-to-be-realized potential and the manifestation of where you want to be in the days and years to come. You start trekking toward your chosen mountain range, and now it's time to choose your specific mountain peak.

While writing this book, I had the opportunity to climb the largest freestanding mountain in the world—Mt. Kilimanjaro in Tanzania,

Africa. In many ways, business is like this monumental challenge. It will be one of the hardest things you've ever done, but it will also be exhilarating. There will be several routes to the top and you will have many people join the expedition, including guides, fellow adventurers, and porters. There will be health checks along the way and when you reach the top, the experience will change you. But before you can make the summit, you have to identify which mountain you want to start climbing in the first place—a mountain that will represent you and your business evolving into something truly grand.

Not Just a Mountain, But a Path

For example, there are about twenty named routes on Mt. Everest (although 97 percent of climbers end up choosing one of two).[3] The two most popular routes, the South Col and the Northeast Ridge, each comes with pluses and minuses. South Col has a beautiful trek to base camp, easy access to villages, the potential for helicopter rescue, and a slightly warmer, less windy climb. But there's icefall instability, crowds, and longer exposure and night summiting times. The Northeast Ridge is less crowded, has a drivable base camp, is easier to climb to the mid-level camps, and has a shorter summit at night. But the temperatures are colder, it's windier, the camps are at higher elevations, there are more loose rocks, and there's no opportunity for a helicopter rescue.[4] Just as Everest mountaineers must weigh the pros and cons of the various routes available, so too must the entrepreneur

---

3   Arnette, A. (2020, May 23). A New Route on Everest this Spring? Retrieved August 19, 2020, from www.rei.com/blog/climb/a-new-route-on-everest-this-spring.

4   N/a. (2011, February 24). Comparing the Routes on Everest. Retrieved August 19, 2020, from www.outsideonline.com/1808431/comparing-routes-everest.

not only pick the mountain of their dreams, but pay attention to the
costs and benefits of the route they intend to take.

Dream ~~Big~~ Huge

Some years ago, I was on the top floor in an all-glass office with
a large iconic motorcycle parked in the lobby. One of the most
debonair, well-dressed investors I've ever met, James Clarke, sat
across from me. He had just made an investment of over $100 million
into a company he knew with certain confidence would succeed. I was
lucky to have him as a board member for one of my companies. We
were talking about the direction the company would take and what
the end goal could be. I shared a number that I felt was quite lofty and
asked, "But is that big enough?"

He looked back at me and replied, "In our companies we don't dream
big; we dream *huge*." Everything James touches seems to turn to gold
and, in that moment, I began to understand why—he chooses to play
in the major leagues instead of the neighborhood ballpark. He has
massive vision.

One of the first pitfalls most entrepreneurs make is not having a
vision of where their company is going. The second is not dreaming
big enough. Every one of us gets to choose our path and how we
spend our time. If I asked you how many hours Elon Musk (world's
most innovative man), Bill Gates (world's most philanthropic man),
Marissa Mayer (first female CEO of Yahoo) have in their respective
days, what would you say? The answer is the same: twenty-four. All
of us have been blessed with twenty-four hours every day. As Gandalf
the wizard said in J. R. R. Tolkien's *Fellowship of the Ring*, "All we
have to decide is what to do with the time that is given us."

Will you spend your twenty-four hours climbing a small mountain? Will you climb a *huge* mountain? Will you blast off beyond the mountains and send people to Mars? Elon Musk made a choice to be an entrepreneur, and he made the choice to send humans far into space. Think about that…*Elon Musk is going to Mars.* Now that's dreaming *huge*.

What is *your* potential? What is the company's potential? It's time to unleash yourself and dream big, because you get to decide how big your company is going to be. Now, you may think there are things outside of your control and you can't determine the future. For now, take a leap of faith, because Overcoming Pitfall 4 will help get you past those fears. I love the words of the great Wayne Gretzky, "You miss 100 percent of the shots you never take." What goal will you put your twenty-four hours toward?

From Dreams to Goals

Dreams are about vision; goals are about action. Execution is what sets apart those who achieve their goals and those who stay dreamers. The route to success is through daily action on a predetermined plan.

You may dream of climbing the mountain, but without effective goal setting, you'll never make it all the way to the top. Remember that goals are:[5]

- Only achievable if they have been articulated first.

- 42 percent more likely to be achieved if you write them down.

- Stronger if accompanied by a commitment to action.

---

5 The Science Behind Setting Goals (and Achieving Them). (2019, February 26). Retrieved August 20, 2020, from forbesbooks.com/the-science-behind-setting-goals-and-achieving-them; Goodman, N. (2018, December 16). The science of setting goals. Retrieved August 20, 2020, from ideas.ted.com/the-science-of-setting-goals.

- More likely to be achieved if the goal setter is accountable
  to others.

- Kept on track through a cadence of regular updates.

- More than just an easy win; they need to be significant.

- Better realized if they focus on the process, not just
  the outcome.

- More powerful if framed positively versus negatively.

- Subject to setbacks, so prepare for it and make learning part
  of the plan.

Remember that you get to choose your direction, your peak, and your route. You can choose the million-dollar peak, or the fifty-million-dollar peak. You can pick the harder bushwhacking route or the trail which has been trod before. You can choose to climb the mountain in three, five, seven, or ten days. In my Africa mountaineering experience, we chose the five-day path called the Marangu route. It is one of the faster routes, has huts instead of camps, and has some of the best views along the forty-four-mile round trip. We could have chosen a slower route to help us acclimate easier and make the trip a little more enjoyable, but we believed we could make this journey, and so we embarked. Your journey is up to you. There are many routes up the mountain, and each has its own benefits: some are shorter distance but tougher climbing, some take longer but are easier on the body. The beauty is you get to choose the route that's best for you, and this chapter will show you how.

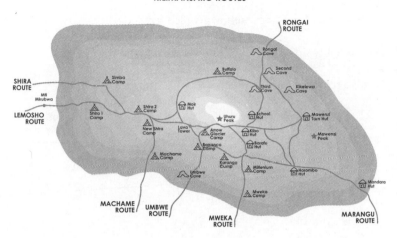

KILIMANJARO ROUTES

AMBITION transforms into a GOAL when paired with a written date. A GOAL morphs into a PLAN when sliced into accountable steps. A PLAN translates into SUCCESS when implemented with daily ACTION.

To give yourself the best chance of success in turning your dreams into reality, you will need to set specific and realistic goals that are inspiring. Many people use an effective goal setting process called SMART Goals, and there's a good chance you've heard this acronym before. SMART Stands for Specific, Measurable, Attainable, Relevant, and Time-based. I have my clients create SMART-I goals adding "Inspiration" to the end. SMART-I Goals are aspirational, ignite our passion, and are worthy of being celebrated at the end. Using this format, you will find each of these elements encapsulated in four key areas specific to entrepreneurial goals:

- Event Goal (IPO, Acquisition, Market Dominance, etc.)

- Monetary Goal (Revenue, Profitability, Market Dominance, etc.)

- Time Goal (Month and Year)

- Impact Goal (the result in people's lives)

Or in other words, *How much by when for what and why?*

Here's a template (and remember to be as specific as possible):

My company will reach $_____ in revenue by (month and year) _____ when we will (event)_____ which will (impact) _____.

Here are some examples:

Lifestyle Company

My company will reach two million dollars in revenue by (month and year) October 2030 when I will (what event?) be personally and professionally debt-free, which will (huge goal) allow me to pay off my house, travel the world with my family, and give me more time to write my novel.

Buy or Be Bought

My company will reach $31 million in revenue by (month and year) April 2031 when I will (what event?) have an equity event at a 3.34x valuation which will (huge goal) provide complete financial freedom for myself and family for generations to come. It will also provide the means to start a nonprofit foundation to help immigrants start businesses and earn their citizenship.

IPO

My company will reach $250 million in revenue by (month and year) October 2035 when we will (what event?) IPO with an initial offering of twenty million shares opening at twenty-one dollars per share, which will (huge goal) give me the ability to purchase a professional sports franchise.

Set your sights high, climb to the top of that peak, celebrate, and then look up for your next adventure. If you're not sure your goal is realistic, keep reading the next chapter: Overcoming Pitfall 3: Pulling a Goal out of Thin Air.

Overcoming Pitfall 2: Create the Map/Make the Plan

There are many ways to choose your destination. To help you dream big, here is a template:

- Determine which **mountain range** you are going to climb.

    - Lifestyle

    - Buy or Be Bought (Acquisition)

    - IPO

- Pick your specific **mountain** by completing the formula for an actionable goal above—*How much | by when | for what | and why (your huge goal)?*
  My company will reach $_____ in revenue by (month and year) _____ when we will (what event?)_____ which will (huge goal) _____.

- Register your goal on the website for additional accountability and reporting at EntrepreneursParadox.com/AccurateGoal. We will help you achieve your goals.

- Note: I highly recommend you determine your mountain
  range and pick your mountain now. Doing so will help you get
  the most out of the remaining chapters. And don't worry about
  getting it "right" or not. The following chapters will guide you
  through validating your goals.

Pitfall 3

Pulling a Goal Out of Thin Air

Some entrepreneurs pull goals out of thin air. The ones who create theirs from solid data are the ones who don't have to question the validity of their goals.

A typical pitfall that entrepreneurs encounter early is setting goals without having gone through the process of reverse engineering them and making sure they are sound. Like any expert climber, you must properly plan for the journey—especially for a trip of this magnitude. Consider some of the critical questions a climber needs to ask and answer before setting out:

- How many miles is the trip?
- What kind of food is important to bring?
- What clothes, coats, and shoes will I need?
- How much moleskin will I need to cover my blisters?
- Will I need oxygen?
- What other supplies do I need?
- Where will we camp overnight? What shelter do we need?
- Which route will I take up the mountain?

- How long will it take to reach the summit?

- How will I train for the expedition?

- Who will be joining me on this adventure?

- How do I hire a guide for the ascent?

- What will the celebration look like at the top?

Without proper planning, you could get halfway up the mountain and end up having to turn around for any number of reasons: you could run out of food, have the wrong gear, or even lose track of the path to the top. To ensure the greatest chance of success, the mountain needs to be analyzed and the journey reverse engineered. This applies to the entrepreneur as well, who must reverse engineer the voyage up the business mountain.

The Reverse Engineering Critical Questions

Let's review the previous climbing questions again, only this time through an entrepreneurial lens:

- How many miles is the trip?
  What is your current revenue? What's the difference between where you are now and the revenue goal? Estimate how many products or services you will need to sell to reach this goal.

- What kind of food is important to bring?
  How much cash will you consume in reaching your goal? What is the expected yearly burn rate and total cash outlay to reach the goal?

- What clothes, coats, and shoes will I need?
  What will your company look like when you hit your goal?

How will the brand be represented? What articles and press releases will you launch? What will be your reach and market penetration? How will people perceive your brand and what brand ranking will your company need to achieve to hit your goal?

- How much moleskin will I need to cover my blisters? Write out the difficulties you expect to encounter along the way. What obstacles will you need to overcome? What equipment will you likely need to replace along the way?

- Will I need oxygen? Do you expect to make a large purchase of technologies or acquire other companies to reach your goal? Will you need an infusion of cash at some point up the mountain? Do you plan to expand internationally? Are you going to run a Super Bowl ad or dominate the market with advertising? If you answered yes to any of these, where will the money come from? Will you self-fund from the profits of the company? Will you seek additional funding: venture capital, private equity, debt financing, friends and family, angel investors, crowdfunding, personal savings, or a strategic partner?

- What other supplies do you need? What is your required list of equipment? If your company deals entirely in virtual goods or services, list out all the computers, desks, chairs, phones, etc.

- Where will we camp overnight? What shelter do we need? How many locations or markets do you need to be in to achieve the goal? How many offices or buildings will you need?

- Which route will I take up the mountain? Plan the ascent up the mountain year-by-year. Plan what the revenue per year increase will look like. Plan how many people you need to hire and when. Determine when you must move into your new office space. Plan for any acquisitions or purchases of technology or intellectual property. Do it year-by-year all the way up to the month you reach your goal.

- How long will it take you to reach the summit?
  Is it six years, ten years, or three years? This is best determined by first discovering the revenue number, growth rate, and number of units sold. Once you have a clear vision around these items, you can confidently estimate a timeframe.

- How will I train for the expedition?
  What skills do you, as the CEO, need to have to accomplish your goal? How will you get that training? How will your current and future team get the skills they need?

- Who will join you on this adventure?
  When you hit your goal, how many people will be working at your company? Lay out the org chart. Use your current production rates to determine the number of people needed to produce the product or deliver the service. Add in sales, marketing, and customer support departments. Add in key roles for HR, operations, and finance. Will you bring legal in-house? If you feel like you are taking a stab in the dark about how many people you will have when you hit your goal, you can reverse engineer this as well by working backward from "revenue per employee" (RPE). For example, if you have a goal of $10 million and your rev/employee is $400,000, that equals twenty-five employees. Here is a chart that displays RPE by industry of S&P 500. Startups in growth mode are going to be in the $150,000-$400,000 range.

EMPLOYEE REVENUE PER MILLION

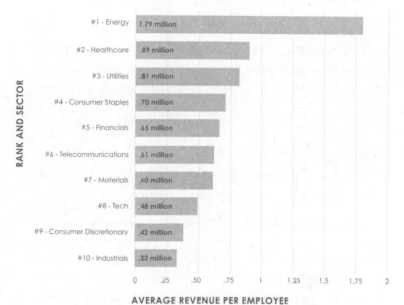

AVERAGE REVENUE PER EMPLOYEE

Source: https://craft.co/reports/s-p-500-revenue-per-employee-perspective

- How do I hire a guide for the ascent?
  Who has experience creating successful ventures? Ask that
  person to mentor you, or hire a coach. There's no need to make
  the mistakes other climbers have made—a coach or mentor
  will help you avoid such pitfalls.

- What will the celebration look like at the top?
  How will I celebrate my victory when I finally summit? Do
  something big to celebrate, like taking the entire company on
  a Caribbean cruise with everyone's families. Or celebrate by
  getting the payday you've been working for. Sell the company
  to your largest competitor or a private equity group and make
  sure you celebrate personally as well as with a reward and party
  for the company.

Perform a Reality Check

Now that you've laid out your plans in intricate detail, let's do a reality check by looking at others who have climbed the mountain and see how things measure up. Let's assume an expected growth rate of $3 million to $30 million in six years. The formula for growth rate is:

([Present—Past] / Past) * 100

We will calculate as if the "Present" is at the end of the goal and "Past" is today. So in our scenario, the growth rate when we reach the goal would be:

([$30,000,000—$3,000,000]/$3,000,000) *100 = 900 percent

This is a 900 percent growth over ten years. How does that play out year-over-year if we lay it out linearly? Growth is rarely in a straight line, but for these purposes it helps to illustrate what it looks like:

Revenue	YoY Growth Rate	Cumulative Growth Rate	Three-Year Growth Rate
$3,000,000	0	0	0
$6,000,000	100.0%	100.0%	0
$9,000,000	50.0%	200.0%	0
$12,000,000	33.3%	300.0%	300.0%
$15,000,000	25.0%	400.0%	150.0%
$18,000,000	20.0%	500.0%	100.0%
$21,000,000	16.7%	600.0%	75.0%
$24,000,000	14.3%	700.0%	60.0%
$27,000,000	12.5%	800.0%	50.0%

Revenue	YoY Growth Rate	Cumulative Growth Rate	Three-Year Growth Rate
$30,000,000	11.1%	900.0%	42.9%
Average	31.4%	500.00%	86.43%

This is an average growth rate of 31.4 percent. So how does this compare to other growth stories? The following chart reflects the median growth rate of publicly traded companies in the major markets over the last ten years from the time of this writing.

"Dow Jones: The Dow Jones Industrial Average tracks thirty large, publicly owned blue-chip companies trading on the New York Stock Exchange (NYSE) and the NASDAQ."

"NASDAQ: The NASDAQ composite was created by the National Association of Securities Dealers (NASD) on February 8, 1971. The NASDAQ Exchange is mostly composed of more than three thousand stocks of the world's leading tech and biotech leaders like Comcast, Apple, Netflix, PayPal, Google, Microsoft, Oracle, Amazon, and Intel."

"Annualized Growth Rate: The yearly average increase in the total value of an individual investment."

"Blue Chip: A blue chip is a nationally recognized, well-established, and financially sound company. Blue chips generally sell high-quality, widely accepted products and services. Blue-chip companies are known to weather downturns and operate profitably in the face of adverse economic conditions, which helps to contribute to their long record of stable and reliable growth."

Annualized Growth Rates		
Dow Jones	**S&P500**	**NASDAQ**
9.70%	11.33%	18.46%

These numbers represent large blue-chip companies, which are
different from where you are, so there are a couple of other indices we
need to consider. Companies in their first ten years have the potential
to grow much faster than the publicly traded markets listed above.
According to data gathered from *Inc. Magazine*, the average three-
year growth rate for the five thousand fastest growing companies
in the US is 155 percent. This compares to our scenario very well.
Our average three-year growth rate is 86.43 percent, which is very
conservative for a new start-up. The chart below shows the median
growth rates of private companies listed on the *Inc. Magazine*'s.
500/5000 index for the last six years. It also has the top fifty fastest
growing privately held companies so you can see how the very top
performers do.

Year	Growth Rate (Median)	Top 50
2020	165%	9127%
2019	158%	7453%
2018	172%	9154%
2017	142%	9339%
2016	143%	7684%
2015	150%	8123%
Six-Year Avg	**155%**	**8578%**

But let's get a little more specific. Here are the numbers broken down into several industries for the last six years, including how the top twenty-five performed. Pick your industry and see how your three-year growth plan measures up to how these fast-growing companies are experiencing rapid growth. For the most recent data go to EntrepreneursParadox.com/GrowthRate.

Industry	Median Growth	Top Twenty-Five
Advertising/Marketing	171%	6586%
Agriculture & Natural Resources	159%	N/A
Business Products and Services	136%	2114%
Computer Hardware	161%	200%
Construction	146%	942%
Consumer Products & Services	187%	2402%
Education	156%	1290%

Industry	Median Growth	Top Twenty-Five
Engineering	124%	575%
Environmental Services	135%	202%
Financial Services	150%	1868%
Food & Beverage	176%	1201%
Government Services	197%	898%
Health	169%	2598%
Human Resources	118%	898%
Insurance	131%	357%
IT Management	129%	940%
IT Services	112%	N/A
IT System Development	182%	842%
Logistics & Transportation	154%	1690%
Manufacturing	115%	659%
Media	217%	461%
Real Estate	170%	1060%
Retail	224%	1929%
Security	185%	349%
Software	183%	3129%
Telecommunications	134%	434%
Travel & Hospitality	153%	355%

For an updated and comprehensive list of all industries, go to:
EntrepreneursParadox.com/CompareGrowthRates.

If you are really dreaming big, here is another piece of data to
compare against: the fastest growth to one billion dollars:

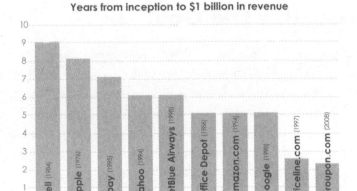

Years from inception to $1 billion in revenue

Sources: Capital IQ, a Standard & Poor's business; Morgan Stanley;
Thomson Reuters Fundamentals via FactSet Research Systems; Forbes.

Don't Pull Numbers Out of Thin Air

Do your research. The two most common responses I hear from
entrepreneurs when I do this exercise are: "I want my company
to grow to $50 million or $100 million" and "I want to do it

in five years." Make sure you're not just pulling numbers out
of thin air. Walk through this exercise by going to the website
(EntrepreneursParadox.com/CompareGrowthRates) and enter your
actual numbers so you can have a realistic, feasible, and motivational
goal. Evaluate where you're at today and what it will take to get you
to where you want to be. Is your plan realistic based on comparables,
growth rates, and the number of units you would need to sell to
achieve your goal? Rework the numbers until you believe them
wholeheartedly. You own this. You may feel a bigger potential than
what others are doing, and that's great. Use this as the baseline and
then go with your gut.

Visualize the Goal

The purpose of this exercise is not just for planning—you need to be
able to close your eyes and vividly picture the day you accomplish
your goal. You need to be able to visualize where you are in the office
and see, feel, and smell the environment and events as they take
place. Don't dismiss the power of this undertaking. In fact, give it a
try right now. Put the book down, or press pause if you're listening
to the audio version. Picture yourself and your surroundings at the
end point of your journey as viscerally as possible. Did you see it?
If not, fill in the details even further, then close your eyes again and
create this picture as if you are actually there. This may take a few
attempts before you start to see the details and colors of the room,
but it is important that you can see the friends who took the journey
with you, feel the hands you're shaking, and taste the celebratory cake.
Practice this visualization repeatedly, especially in the morning before
getting ready for the day. Cement the image in your mind until it's all
but inevitable.

"YoY: Year-Over-Year (YoY) is a frequently used financial comparison for comparing two or more measurable events on an annualized basis. Looking at YoY performance allows for gauging if a company's financial performance is improving, static, or worsening."

Overcoming Pitfall 3: Reverse Engineer the Goal

- Go to the website and calculate your desired growth rate for your company. You can put in the final revenue numbers or your Year-over-Year (YoY) growth rate, which it will calculate for you. EntrepreneursParadox.com/CalculateGrowthRate.

- Go to the website and compare your growth rate to the most up-to-date stats for growth rates of other companies in your industry. EntrepreneursParadox.com/CompareGrowthRates.

- Write out your goals in detail following each bullet point as shown in the chapter.

- Go to the website and enter your data to get a visual representation of your goal in infographic format. EntrepreneursParadox.com/GoalInfographic.

Pitfall 4

Trusting Your Fears

We are only born with two innate fears. Everything else is learned...and can be unlearned.

Here is a test that you'll likely face as an entrepreneur: As you journey up your inspiring mountain, there are no benches, signs, or handrails. This is *your* path to the top—a trail that is uniquely yours. But along the way, a thought crosses your mind: *What if I can't make it to the top?* You keep pushing forward but a little slower than before as another doubt creeps into your head: *What if I fail? How can I let down everyone counting on me?* The pace slows again. *What if I don't have what it takes?* These speculative distortions have now stopped you in your tracks and, instead of focusing on the future and your goal, you are fixated on ways not to fail. Just a few doubts managed to shift your purpose from the triumph of conquering the mountain to self-preservation. Fear is the doorway to distortion. You are no longer playing to win; you are simply playing not to lose. Fear stops people in their tracks.

The crazy thing is that fear is nearly 100 percent imagined—it is a trick of the mind. A pivotal study done by scientists in the 1960s found there are only two innate fears we are born with: the fear of falling (basophobia) and a fear of loud noises (acoustic startle reflex).[6] Infants weren't scared of creepy crawlies or public speaking or any of the fears we call "natural fears." That spider or snake that makes your skin crawl is an acquired fear. The anxiety of speaking or performing in front of a crowd is developed as we grow. A fear of a needle, drowning, darkness, flying, and tight spaces are all learned.

As entrepreneurs, we have our own unique set of fears, which can include:

- Financial security

- Ability to fund the venture

- Personal ability/self-esteem (Imposter Syndrome)

- Potential of the idea

- Threats to social esteem

6   Gibson, E. J., & Walk, R. D. (1960). The "visual cliff." *Scientific American*, 202, 67–71.

- The venture's executability

- Opportunity costs

I find solace in the fact that almost all entrepreneurs face the same fears. It's a lot easier when you realize it isn't just you—it's practically everyone who starts a business. How many of the above fears can you relate to? Do you constantly worry about how you are going to make the next payroll? Do you worry people are going to learn you don't know what you are doing? Are you worried that everything you are doing is fake?

Don't worry, it is very normal to have these fears, and this chapter will provide you with some tools to combat and overcome them. The beauty of all but two fears being learned is that all fear is a construct of the mind. This means all fears when addressed properly can be overcome. The way we do this is by looking at fear with truth.

"Perplexing on the past produces pain.
Fretting on the future fuels fear.
Only the present provides peace and power."

—RICHARD VASS

On Kilimanjaro, there are several routes to the top, some more comfortable a climb than others. Addressing fear is not a comfortable route; but the beauty is Fear Falters when Faced.

The One Letter That Changes Fear into Power

Language is one of the most powerful tools in our personal arsenal to change our future. A single letter *S* can help you transform fear into power.

Evaluate these two phrases:

What if… What is…

What If fuels fear, creates stories and distortions, and can start a downward spiral.

What Is leads to being present in the moment, creates ownership of the problem, lives in truth, dispels distortion, and creates ownership and responsibility.

There is only a one-letter difference, and yet the diverging roads from each are polar opposites of each other. By evaluating *What Is* in the current moment versus *What If* bad things happen in the future, the holder of these thoughts changes fear, uncertainty, and doubt into power. As Shakespeare penned in *Julius Caesar*, "Cowards die many times before their deaths. The valiant never taste of death but once."

Evaluate how you feel when you read the following *What If* statements:

"What if…I mess up this presentation?"

"What if…I launch this product and nobody buys it?"

"What if…I go bankrupt?"

"What if…I train my employees and they leave or try to compete?"

"What if…my team doesn't like me?"

"What if…people find out I really don't know how to start a business?"

"What if…I spend $30,000 on a website redesign and I don't see any ROI?"

"What if…someone thinks I'm incompetent?"

"What if…I'm not good enough, fast enough, smart enough, strong enough, or even just enough?"

Did you experience tension in your chest? Did you feel nervous or anxious? I've had all of these thoughts and worries as an entrepreneur, and nearly all entrepreneurs feel the same way. Whenever you hear yourself saying these sentences in your mind or whenever you feel this type of anxiety, swap the letter "f" for an "s" and see what happens. Here are some of the power statements within "What is…"

"What is…my goal?"

"What is…my responsibility in the situation?"

"What is…the one thing (the first thing) I can do today to progress toward my goal?"

"What is…in my power to change?"

"What is…the truth?"

"What is…important right now?"

"What is…the opportunity cost if I don't take action?"

"What is…the path I choose to take?"

"What is…my opportunity in this trial?"

"What is…a third alternative I haven't thought of yet?"

"What is…the next step?"

Notice the difference in how you felt? My guess is you felt empowered, ready to face the challenge, excited, and maybe even exhilarated. Fear is a liar because it tries to get us to believe we aren't capable and that life is outside of our control. Fear puts us in a fixed mindset that paralyzes us along our journey to the top of the mountain. How often do we delve into those fears and let them control our thinking, or worse, debilitate our actions?

Seneca may have put it best:

> *"There is only one way to happiness and that is to cease worrying about things which are beyond the power of our will."*

I was lucky enough to coach Scott Severe, who was continually worried his company's software and app were not able to keep up with a competitor. The competitor was the largest in the industry and Scott was trying to compete by adding developers, money, and resources to build the most feature-rich app possible. He feared that his offering was not as good and his company would lose clients and market share if they didn't keep adding tools and features like their competitor. The trouble was, ninety percent of all expenses were being spent on the development team salaries and technology. They kept asking, "*What if* we don't keep up? *What if* we don't have the best technology? *What if* we don't have the latest and greatest features?"

I challenged his fears by asking him *What Is* questions.

Q: "What is the offering in its current iteration?"
A: "A pretty good product."

Q: "What is the minimum viable product?"
A: "We've already achieved it."

Q: "What is the worst that would happen to sales if you stopped developing today?"
A: "Probably nothing."

Q: "What is the longest you could go without adding another feature and still get clients?"
A: "Probably a year, maybe a year and a half."

Q: "What is the best use of your money/revenue right now?"
A: "Using our money to make more money."

Q: "What is the shortest route to more revenue?"
A: "Adding salespeople."

After several *What Is* questions, it was decided Scott would take the money he was going to spend on future development and hire salespeople instead. The decision was clear. The software *is* good enough in its current version. New clients wouldn't even notice if new features weren't rolled out for a year or more, and current clients weren't complaining about missing features. Scott's company focused their efforts on ways to make more money instead of developing an endless array of *What If* questions and ended up doubling revenue in one year! The competitor he was worried about keeping up with was so impressed by the sudden jump in revenue they decided to buy Scott's company.

Changing the letter *f* to the letter *s* transforms your entire perspective on the reality of life in the present moment. It brings focus to the *now* and replaces all of those stomach-churning moments with a sense of determination and safety because you choose to take control. The truth that annihilates fear is that you have control of your choices in every situation. This is true even in the most extreme situation, as the case of Archie Williams illustrates. Archie was a recent contestant on the television show *America's Got Talent*. The fifty-nine-year-old had spent the last thirty-seven years in prison based on a wrongful conviction and dreamed of the day he would sing on that stage. Even locked behind bars, he retained the power to choose, telling the panel of celebrity judges, "I knew I was innocent. I didn't commit a crime. But being a poor Black kid, I didn't have the economic ability to fight the state of Louisiana…I was sentenced to life and eighty years without the possibility of parole or probation." But that didn't mean Williams was surrendering to his fate or a fear of the future. "I never let my mind go to prison," he declared. He embraced music and found ways to challenge himself and grow despite being incarcerated. Then, the Innocence Project took up his case, and he was exonerated and released in 2019. Williams achieved his goal of singing on the popular show—a show he'd watched in prison and would dream about one day taking a part in. His story, while heartbreaking, shows the power of the human spirit to take up *What Is* and let go of *What If*, even in the most dire of circumstances.

The next time you are feeling worried or anxious, I invite you to take a good hard look at the *What If*s you are telling stories about and change them into *What Is* truths about the present moment, the choices you have, and your responsibility in it. This simple technique has saved me and many budding entrepreneurs from the paralyzing nature of fear and allowed us to get back to work.

The "What Is" Process for Overcoming Fear

Let's dive deeper into the power of *What Is* thinking by applying specific steps to overcoming fear.

- **Step One: Name the fear**. When you ignore or run from fear, it grows. Fear feeds on fear, including the fear of itself. Don't let fear feed on anything else in your life. Take action to stop it now and fight it with truth, light, and strength. This step takes vulnerability and humility, so let's get vulnerable. Write down your fears. For example, if your goal is to reach $30 million in ten years, write down what scares you about that goal. Sometimes just naming your fear brings it into the light enough that this step alone will alleviate the concern. Say it out loud, write it down, and share it with someone you trust, such as a mentor, coach, or fellow entrepreneur.

Fears

I'm scared I won't make the goal, and everyone will see me fail.

I'm scared I will run out of money.

I'm kind of afraid I'll succeed. I've never had money at that level, and I don't know how it will change my life.

I won't get funding.

I'm scared I will ruin people's lives if I fail because I will have to fire them.

I'm not smart enough to run a $30 million business.

Write your own:

_____

_____

_____

_____

_____

_____

- **Step Two: Identify the Distortions.** Bring the light of truth to dispel the shadows of fear. This step is also best done with a mentor, coach, or trusted friend. Ask them what they see as the truth regarding the fears you've listed. Sometimes we tell ourselves distortions so much, it is hard to distinguish what is true. Do this step with someone who can help you step out of your own head and reveal the distortions. The fact that you have fears is valid because you are exploring a place you've never been before. The fears themselves are not.

Fear	Distortion or Truth	What Is the Truth?
I don't make the goal, and everyone sees me fail.	Distortion	You don't know fully what you are capable of because you haven't yet tried. The only real failure is not trying.
I will run out of money.	Distortion	The truth is over thirty million small businesses in America are making it work and are NOT running out of money. So can you.
I'm afraid I'll succeed because I've never had money at that level, and I don't know how it will change my life.	Truth but the fear is distorted	You may not have had this kind of money. Money acts as a magnifier. Whatever traits and strengths you have now, it will magnify. If you are charitable, you will give more. If you like to play and have fun, you will play bigger. Money magnifies who you are, so be the best person you can be, and money will enhance the good you do in this world.
I won't get funding.	Distortion	You may not get it on your first, second, or even third attempt, but to say you won't ever get it is distortion. In 2018 and 2019 venture capital surpassed $135 billion in the US alone.[7] There is plenty of money to be raised.
I will ruin people's lives if I fail because I will have to fire them.	Distortion	People are resilient. Even though the initial shock might sting, oftentimes getting laid off is a great thing for a person. I started my first venture after my entire team at Ancestry.com got laid off. I was so grateful they gave me the little boost I needed to jump out on my own.
I'm not smart enough to run a $30MM business.	Distortion	You started a business. This fact alone shows you have the courage and dedication to do what it takes to run a successful business at many levels. You will have to transform yourself along the way, but there is no reason you can't run a $30 million business.

7   PitchBook. (2020, January 14). US Venture Capital Investment Surpasses $130 Billion in 2019 for Second Consecutive Year. Retrieved August 20, 2020, from www.prnewswire.com/news-releases/us-venture-capital-investment-surpasses-130-billion-in-2019-for-second-consecutive-year-300986237.html.

Write your own:

Fear	Distortion or Truth	What Is the truth?

- **Step Three: Write out all the "What Is" statements.** Focus on the things you can control rather than worrying about what you can't. For example, how can you prepare for a failure before it happens? What is in your power to eliminate or at least lessen the effects of this outcome? What is in your control if the worst-case scenario happens? What can you do to fix the problem if it occurs? What is the full set of consequences if the least desirable outcome happens?

What if...?	What Is...Controllable	What Is...Fixable
I don't make the goal and everyone sees me fail?	• I get to choose every action and strategy. • I can stack the deck in my favor by getting mentors and peers. • I can transition from being a product builder to becoming a business builder. • I can implement systems to streamline the company's effectiveness. • I can tap into proven business systems and strategies to catapult the business forward.	• I will be grateful for the lessons I've learned and can start over a little smarter.
I run out of money?	• I can learn to manage cash flow effectively. • I can hire an accountant. • I can get funding. • I can extend payables.	• I can get a loan. • I can downsize and reduce expenses. • I can figure out a plan with team members.
I succeed and having money changes my life in negative ways?	• I can evaluate my life and see what I value and what money will magnify. • I can make a plan of how I will spend my money now, so I don't have to worry about it in the future. • I can hire a financial advisor and wealth manager.	• I can make the choice every day of how to use my money. My wealth doesn't define me.
I don't get funding?	• I can build relationships with VCs early before I need funding. • I can understand the most important KPIs for investors (see Pitfall 10). • I can create a killer presentation with this data. • I can build my company in a way that is primed for investment.	• I can try again. • I can hire a broker to shop my company to multiple VCs around the country.

What if...?	What Is...Controllable	What Is...Fixable
I ruin people's lives if I fail and I have to fire them?	• I can hire people only when the numbers work and the company can maintain profitability. • I can hire the best people to create an efficient workforce for less overall cost.	• I can proactively reach out to my network and help team members find jobs. • I can continue to care about them and their families even if they no longer work at my company.
I'm not smart enough to run a $30 million business?	• I can read books. • I can hire a coach. • I can listen to podcasts. • I can work with mentors. • I can grow with my business.	• I can try again once I have the knowledge I was lacking the first time.

Write your own:

What if...?	What Is...Controllable	What Is...Fixable

- **Step Four: Ask yourself where an attempt puts you on the mountain.**
  Your goal as an entrepreneur is to summit the mountain. Imagine if you happen to fall short of the goal—where on the mountain will you be? If you're really struggling with this

one, then embrace the worst-case scenario: if you don't make
it to the top, could you lose everything? Yes, potentially. Is it
likely that you will lose everything and be living in a cardboard
box (or van) down by the river? No. A more likely worst-case
scenario is that you'll be at the base of the mountain again, just
like you were when you started your crazy adventure. Some of
the most successful entrepreneurs I know "failed" in at least
one of their business ventures. So the worst-case scenario is
you are back at the beginning with another chance to start
climbing again. The most likely scenario is that you will end up
some distance up the mountain. It may be halfway or three-
quarters of the way up the mountain, and that's a lot farther
than if you'd never tried. In our expedition, two climbers never
made it to Uhuru Peak, the highest summit of Kilimanjaro, but
we did all make it to Gillman's Point, which is the first summit
of the big mountain. Even though some had to go back down
because of altitude sickness, they still made it 98 percent of
the way. They still had transformational adventures; they still
achieved things they never knew they were capable of.

So, the most likely (and even worst) cases aren't so bad after
all. If your goal is to get to $30 million in revenue and you hit
$20 million with all your efforts, that's an amazing result. If
your goal is to be purchased for a 4x multiple and you hit a
2.5x multiple, you still have quite a phenomenal outcome. If
you want to be in the top ten fastest growing companies in
your state and end up in the top fifty, you are still one of the
fastest growing companies in your state. Making the decision
to go on this journey means you will progress up the mountain
and end up at a higher elevation than you are right now. Plus,
you will gain experience, knowledge, relationships, and the
kind of confidence you can only get by experiencing this kind
of adventure firsthand. Before I climbed Kilimanjaro, I had
three friends at totally different times tell me, you can't go up
the mountain without coming down changed. This is the same
as with you and your business expedition. Take a minute and
walk through those fears and look at "where on the Mountain"
you will be even if you don't reach the summit.

Where on the Mountain?

I gained substantial knowledge.

I created an amazing network of peers, team members, mentors, and customers.

I created something really fun.

I provided several families with an income for *x* amount of time.

I have experience to learn from and build from.

Write your own:

- **Step Five: The opportunity cost of *What If?*** If the fear of *What If* is keeping you from the journey to the top of the mountain, explore where the What If path you're on will eventually take you. What is the opportunity cost of you not attempting the climb? Where will you be financially, emotionally, socially, or physically? What happens to you in a month, three months, six months, a year, or five years down the road? In the end, we only regret the opportunities we didn't take. Don't let the opportunity pass you by. If it can be done, it can be done by you. There is no one better to make this happen and your time is now. Grab hold of your future and start the journey.

The Path of What If...

What will be the outcome and regrets if you don't strive for your goal?

Today	Future
Self-doubt	Feel major regret
Less income	Experience significantly less income
Loss of motivation	Question what could have been
No growth	Become stymied

Write your own:

_____

_____

_____

_____

_____

Remember, fear is a liar. Fear is the counterfeit of faith. Fear and faith both live in the future. One leads you upward with courage, the other leads you down and makes you feel like crap. Have faith in yourself, your team, your idea, and your product. Faith, just like fear, boils down to choices within your control.

Fear and the Brain

A final note about fear: our brain chemistry changes when we're afraid, making it harder to make cognitive decisions. Just like the fear of falling and loud noises is hard-wired, we have an evolutionary response to fear that moves us quickly to a fight-or-flight mode. Our body gets primed for action at the expense of critical thinking. That happens whether there is an actual threat we're facing or simply the perception of something to be fearful over.

> Decisions done in desperation
> dictate disaster.

Remove fear from your brain before making any major decision, otherwise it will likely lead to disaster. Even if it takes going home and sleeping on it, calling a friend to get another perspective, or journaling to change the fear before making any key company decisions. Studies, including one at the University of Pittsburgh, show that there is a physiological effect of anxiety that disrupts the decision-making process.[8] They found that decisions made under distress actually "unclamped" the neurons in the prefrontal cortex, which is the decision-making portion of the brain. This subgroup of neurons is coded for rule-based decision-making. Desperation decisions can start the death spiral: one desperate decision has negative consequences that lead to the next anxiety-riddled decision and so on, until the company starts to spiral downward.

You will be faced with hard and enormous decisions. It's part of being an entrepreneur. Make these decisions from a centered place. A great technique for removing that sinking feeling is to sit quietly

---

8   Bergland, C. (2016, March 17). How Does Anxiety Short Circuit the Decision-Making Process? Retrieved August 20, 2020, from www.psychologytoday.com/us/blog/the-athletes-way/201603/how-does-anxiety-short-circuit-the-decision-making-process.

and breathe as deeply as possible. Count to five while inhaling, hold it for two to five seconds, and then exhale for another count of five. Deep breathing in this way instantly activates the vagus nerve and the parasympathetic nervous system. This has the effect of lowering blood pressure, slowing heart rate, and calming the mind. With a clear head, pick up the phone and talk through the issue with a trusted friend, mentor, or coach. Know that when you experience this type of compromised critical thinking, it can last up to twenty minutes after a fight-or-flight response, so be wary of what decisions you make and give yourself time to relax and recover.

What If Your Fear Becomes a Reality?

Hopefully through this chapter you've been able to see your fears for what they are—False Evidence Appearing Real. One of the points of this chapter is to illustrate the worst-case scenario and ask, what if it came true? Would you survive? The answer is yes. Do any of the fears you outlined mean you stop eating, breathing, or living? No! The worst-case scenario, in truth, is really not that bad—the business may fail and then you get a chance to start over. Some of the most successful entrepreneurs I know have failed at least once…and it was okay because they picked themselves up and went on to huge success.

Overcoming Pitfall 4: Doubt Your Doubts

1. Take the fear assessment on the website EntrepreneursParadox.com/FearAssessment.

2. Complete the five steps from earlier in the chapter. Print out a version from the website EntrepreneursParadox.com/FearSmashing.

3. Walk through the "Smash Fear Questionnaire."

4. Print out and share your fears with a trusted friend or advisor and ask them for their feedback.

5. With your mountain to climb in front of you, write down your biggest fears in attempting to climb the mountain.

6. Write down your experience in your journal or send yourself an email with these fears listed. Heck, send me an email too at vulnerable@entrepreneursparadox.com. I would love to hear about your fears and how you smashed them with truth.

Pitfall 5

Being Frozen by Imposter Syndrome

When you are done criticizing yourself without any positive outcomes, try a different approach of self love, empathy, and approval and see what happens.

One universal fear of all entrepreneurs is Imposter Syndrome—a phenomenon first introduced in the late '70s. The fear is described as doubting one's accomplishments and being outed as a "fraud." You've likely heard whisperings of the imposter syndrome in your own head, often bundled with feelings of depression, stress, and anxiety. A study conducted by psychologist Pauline Rose Clance and Gail Matthews[9] showed that 70 percent of women and men have experienced imposter syndrome.

9 www.chronicle.com/article/youre-not-fooling-anyone.

IMPOSTER SYNDROME – IT'S NOT JUST YOU

70% of men and women report experiencing Imposter Syndrome.

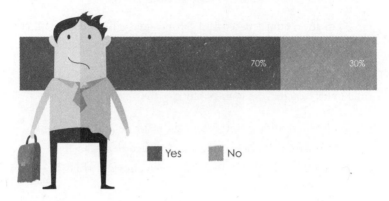

Imposter Syndrome sounds like:

- "If anyone actually knew the truth, they would see I have no idea what I'm doing."

- "I am such a hack/scrub/fake/fraud. I really hope nobody figures out that I am just making this up as I go."

- "I can't let anyone know that I didn't go to school for this. There are so many people who know so much more than I do. Why am I leading this company?"

- "I have to be the expert. I can't let anyone know that I don't have all the answers."

- "Why do I think I can run a company? I've never done this before. As soon as the employees figure out what's REALLY going on, they will quit."

- "They'll soon find out I'm not that great. It's just a matter of time."

- "I'm just lucky. I don't deserve this."

- "Everyone else really seems to have it all together and I have no clue of what's going on."

- "I'm not as capable as they think I am."

- "I'm the leader, I have to have all the answers."

- "I'm always unprepared and getting sideswiped because I don't know what's coming next. I don't know what to plan for."

Do any of these statements resonate with you? Each one creates a mental block to achieving your potential.

The complete definition of imposter syndrome is: "The persistent inability to believe that one's success is deserved or has been legitimately achieved as a result of one's own efforts or skills."

All Entrepreneurs Are Imposters—and That's Okay

When it comes to being an entrepreneur, the truth is you *are* an imposter…in fact, all entrepreneurs are. And that's okay. It's natural and even expected. Think of it this way: no one has ever done what you're doing—in the same way you're doing it, at the time you're doing it, with the same group of customers, etc. You may be walking similar paths as others have in the past along the three mountain ranges, but the journey is uniquely yours. And yet you must travel it as if it was the most familiar terrain in the world as you project strength and act with confidence. Everyone starting your business in the way you're starting it will be an imposter, largely trying to figure it out as they go.

It's tempting to look around and think, *so-and-so is getting write-ups in business magazines and winning awards; they must have it figured out!* Trust me, I was that guy in magazines and buying new trophy shelves for all the awards, and I felt like the biggest imposter of all. In fact, each time I won another award for my business savvy or growth of my company, the imposter syndrome would get deeper. I may have been smiling in the photo, but in my head I was agonizing over how I was going to make payroll the next week.

One of the best ways to overcome imposter syndrome as an entrepreneur is to stop fighting it. Embrace the truth that you're new at this and free yourself from the limiting belief that you have to have it all figured out today. The antidotes to fear are truth and faith. First, be truthful and honest with yourself. Be honest with your team, your family, and with your fellow entrepreneurs. Be truthful in every sense. Fear can be broken down as **False Evidence Appearing Real**. By shining the light of truth on that false evidence, the fear dissipates. It quickly fades into nothing. Once the fear is blasted with the light of truth, replace it with faith.

Recognize there are lots of imposters out there taking refuge behind their shiny masks but secretly agonizing on the inside. It's like the college professor talking over everyone's head while you slump in your chair and think, *I must be stupid—I'm the only one who doesn't get this because nobody else has raised their hand.* Then, when someone does raise their hand and asks a question, there's an almost audible sigh of relief from the rest of the class. Turns out you were all in the same boat and everyone was struggling.

This same phenomenon is happening in your community of fellow start-up founders right now. No one wants to look like they're mentally slower than the rest of the class, and so everyone stays quiet. Instead, be the person who breaks the silence; raise your hand and ask questions. Stop pretending you have to have all the answers because you don't, and it's okay that you don't. We're all entrepreneurial imposters, sitting on our hands and hoping our discomfort doesn't show. The last thing an entrepreneur needs is all that unnecessary stress and pressure—there are plenty of other causes to devote time and attention to.

The Seven Imposter Types

1. **The Perfectionist**—Focused on having a perfect product or service, and if any portion is lower than the expectation, then the entire project is deemed a failure by the entrepreneur because it isn't "good enough."

2. **The Expert**—Primarily concerned with what one knows or can do. Because the expectation is to know everything, anything that falls short of that is often seen as a failure.

3. **The Soloist**—If the Expert is concerned about the "what," the Soloist is focused on the "who." They see challenges as something they have to take on themselves, and asking for help as a sign of weakness and failure.

4. **The Superhero**—Measures success by how many difficult tasks and roles they can take on, excel at, and juggle at the same time. Their "kryptonite" is allowing something to fall through the cracks as the veneer of being able to handle everything "with ease" falls away.

5. **The Genius**—The Genius often judges their competence based on the ease and speed with which they can get things done. When a task can't get done quickly, fluently, or correctly the first time, it can evoke feelings of shame. After all, they are expected to possess a "natural" prowess for entrepreneurial endeavors.

6. **The Fortune Teller**—A futurist who likes to look at what the future will hold. The Fortune Teller makes bets on what tech or future innovations will be needed. They hold this ability to be paramount in the success of the business. If anything is not predicted accurately, shame sets in.

7. **Meta-imposter**—Having two or more of these types qualifies the entrepreneur for meta-imposter syndrome. If you are

experiencing the overwhelm of these symptoms, it is time to focus on this. Set this as a priority.

Each one of these imposter types has specific traits that can be overcome by embracing the truth of who you are and where you're at in your business. If you want to dive deeper into the specific types of imposter syndrome and take an assessment to discover which of the seven types of imposter syndrome you relate to most, you can find it at: EntrepreneursParadox.com/ImposterSyndrome

Forget the Label and Keep Climbing

Summiting Mt. Kilimanjaro was an unforgettable experience full of diverse emotions such as joy, pain, doubt, elation, comradery, inspiration, motivation, and stretching beyond what we thought was previously possible. As each day got progressively harder, I started hearing comments from our group like:

"What was I thinking coming here? I'm not a mountain climber."

"I didn't train like everyone else. I'm not sure I can make it."

"Why did I think I could do this? I don't know anything about climbing a mountain."

Parts of each statement were accurate: they weren't professional mountain climbers, they didn't know the perfect way to climb the mountain, they may not have trained like everyone else…and in the end, none of those negative statements mattered. What mattered was the willingness to keep putting one foot in front of the other and progressing upward. Likewise, it doesn't matter what label or title you have, how much you know or don't know, or how much prior training you've received. The single most important factor to making it to the top of the entrepreneurial mountain is putting one foot in front of the other. As the mountain guides would say, "*po-le, po-le* to the top" (slowly, slowly, to the top).

In my experience, when an entrepreneur is vulnerable enough to expose that this is their first (or even second or third) time starting a business and there are many things they don't know, everyone around them starts feeling comfortable enough to open up and say things like, "Yeah, I'm just figuring it out too." That is when the real conversations start, the shiny masks come off, and the truth anesthetizes the fear. Fellow entrepreneurs will feel a bond with you and the people working for you will see you as real and genuine. You can start building a trusted support network of fellow entrepreneurs who are vulnerable enough to admit they can't see the future either and they don't have all the answers. If you are honest and vulnerable with your peers, this group will bond together in ways you can't imagine—you will build each other up, be there to offer to support, and most importantly, learn together at a faster pace than you ever could on your own.

Finally, when your band of travelers reaches your respective summits, celebrate. Sure, you had no idea what you were doing and you did a lot of faking it (also called learning) along the way. You may not have held the title of professional mountain climber, and you probably tripped and even fell several times on your ascent. But because of the struggles and failures, and because it was hard and you still made it, plant your flag and celebrate the victory. Embrace your success regardless of whether anyone (especially your subconscious) thinks you deserve it. The fact is, you reached the summit, so now you get to enjoy the view.

The Power of Self-Belief

The words of Sallie Krawcheck are profound: "If you're not making some notable mistakes along the way, you're certainly not taking enough business and career chances." So why is there an entire chapter about imposter syndrome in a book on entrepreneurship? Because self-belief is the gatekeeper to your goals. Stop worrying about whether or not you are qualified, smart enough, or good enough. Stop caring if you deserve it. It doesn't matter if you deserve it or not. It's there for the taking. Anyone can take the next step and then the one after that. Most don't. That's why the entrepreneur's journey is so magnificent—it's a rare commodity. Each step holds courage, holds greatness, and holds victory. If you keep telling yourself that you are someone who can't make it or doesn't deserve to be at the top of the mountain, you will follow through on that belief. But if you believe you can achieve the goal, you will overcome the fear and turn it into progress. You will stop asking *what if* and start asking *how*.

Believe!

Believe in you—and in the *huge* vision of your future company.

Accept imposter syndrome as a mislabeled attribute that all entrepreneurs face: if all who walk one step after the other along their unique journeys must do so without perfect vision, experience, knowledge, tools, and expertise, then we are all imposters—each one of us. But that does not mean we are doomed to fail. Instead, it grants us the opportunity to embrace hope and honesty, and the humility to stumble and learn, and create networks of support and empowerment. Perhaps to think otherwise is the real imposter syndrome.

Overcoming Pitfall 5: Embrace Your Reality

1. Accept the fact that you are new at this and don't have all the answers, and that it's okay you don't. As the old Buddhist saying goes: "Serenity comes when you trade expectations for acceptance."

2. If you write in a journal, write at least one paragraph of empathy for yourself as an entrepreneur who is starting something new and amazing. If you don't write in a journal, just send an email to yourself with the same info.

3. Write down a list of five fellow entrepreneurs who you respect and admire. Take each of them to lunch and get vulnerable. Express how you are coming to terms with being okay not knowing everything. Let them know you are committing to taking off the "shiny" mask and getting real. Ask them what their shiny mask is and then ask about times when they didn't know what they were doing.

4. If you're feeling up to sharing, send us an email at vulnerable@ entrepreneursparadox.com. I would love to hear how it went when you were vulnerable and what you learned.

5. Go to the website EntrepreneursParadox.com/
    ImposterSyndrome. Take the survey to find out which
    imposter syndrome you have and how to overcome it.

Wearing All the Hats

First, find the right people. Then hyperfocus on the tasks only you as the leader can do and leave the rest to those you trust.

With my first two businesses, I took a weird kind of pride in telling others I was able to wear all the hats myself. I donned the tech genius hat, the innovator hat, the accountant hat, the lawyer hat, the product manager hat, the project manager hat, and even the office custodian hat. I took pride in the fact that *I* could do all the jobs it took to run a business. This was such folly.

What wearing all the hats really meant was I was messing up the books, falling behind on projects, signing contracts that would later get me in trouble, acting as the bottleneck for any new product launch, and forgetting to empty the trash cans so they were overflowing. Because I wore all the hats, my productivity, not to mention my health, suffered. Which isn't to say that the company wasn't having some success, it's just that it was unsustainable and I was falling apart at the seams. Part of all my hat wearing was a false sense of pride that I was both a jack-of-all-trades and that I didn't have to spend money to hire "experts."

You might recognize that same sense of hat-wearing pride when it comes to your own entrepreneurial impulses. You can do it all yourself, right? You're the superhero of this particular story. But imagine climbing a mountain and trying to do all the jobs yourself. You would have to be the mountain climber, medic, cook, porter, guide, and scout, and carry all the supplies. Ridiculous, right? So why is it so easy to pretend this will work in business when it's so obviously out of sync with the requirements of the real world? The takeaway here is important: stop wearing all the hats and start handing them out to others (i.e. hiring). Do this at the first possible opportunity, and I recommend in the following order. Hire or outsource:

- An accountant

- A lawyer

- An assistant

- HR, payroll, and benefits

The Accountant

If you're in business, you're making and spending money. Accountants know how to manage this in the way that's best for your business. The reason hiring an accountant is so critical is you likely have a set of books that, let's just say, aren't very pretty, complete with a drawer full of unexpensed receipts, undeposited checks (less likely), and unrecorded taxes. In addition to getting things cleaned up, an accountant will be able to create a P&L, balance sheet, and cash flow analysis reports. This is a hat that you don't want to wear because it requires an expertise you're probably not very good at. Accept this fact and let it go, even if you're thinking: *I don't want anyone else to know my numbers, can I trust another person with my money?* or *I don't have enough money to hire an accountant.*

If your concern is that you don't want anyone to know your numbers, please go back and reread Pitfall 5: Being Frozen by Imposter

Syndrome, then return to this chapter. If you're having trouble
trusting someone with your money, set up safeguards to protect it.
This is a good idea, regardless of whether you trust someone or not.
Put limits on signing power, set boundaries with the person over what
they'll have access to and what they won't, have an independent audit
each year, and most importantly, learn how to read a balance sheet
and profit and loss statement so that you can have weekly informed
conversations with your accountant. Finally, if you feel you're not
able to afford an accountant, there are now companies and services
where you can rent a fractional CFO or part-time bookkeeper at a
very reasonable rate. I suggest engaging one once a week to start and
then grow as needed. These services get you what you want without
having to retain someone full-time on staff. And don't forget, an
accountant is worth their weight in gold. They will prevent you from
making costly tax mistakes, keep the bills paid on time, and remove
the stress from your life so you can focus on the important parts of
being an entrepreneur. You might be concerned about the expense,
but it will never be as costly as not having your books and taxes in
proper order.

The Lawyer

A lawyer's job is to keep you safe. The sooner you hire a lawyer,
the safer you will be. There is so much to setting up a business that
needs to be done the right way from the start. If you didn't have a
lawyer when you started your company, then ask your lawyer to do
an audit of all the legal docs, including your articles of incorporation,
operating agreement/bylaws, employee agreements, customer-facing
contracts, privacy policies, and any other documents that are used in
your operation. You can put a lawyer on retainer for a pre-defined
number of hours each month or just have an on-call relationship.
Find one who is business savvy and not only understands law but

understands business. Sometimes the best legal solution is not always the best overall solution. When interviewing a lawyer, ask in what increments they charge. If they say they bill in fifteen-minute intervals, not a full hour, you've found a potential match.

The Assistant

An assistant will help you stay organized like you never thought possible. Similar to removing the other two hats, this one can be hired in steps. You can first hire a service to do this for you, including organizing meetings, following up with appointments the day of, coordinating calendars, arranging travel, and getting you to where you need to be on time each day. These services can be affordable and will simplify your life. As things progress and you move into the next stages of your business, you can look to hire an assistant full-time.

HR Outsourcing

As your company grows, you will start bringing on more and more employees. Employees add a whole new dimension and complexity to the business. Before worrying about payroll taxes, benefits packages, insurance, and the other myriad things that come along with employing others, simply hire a payroll and benefits company. Yes, your accountant can do this too, but payroll companies are specifically set up for this. Most of them will take a start-up with only a few employees. The benefit of working with this type of company, especially in the beginning stages, is that they can provide big-company benefits. They're able to aggregate multiple companies under one umbrella and provide benefits you would never be able to give your employees without them. Doing this yourself will consume your time and will be a fairly stressful part of your job. Don't let the distractions overtake the important work you need to do every day. HR outsourcing is a common practice now, and even large companies will use an outsourcing agency instead of bringing it in house.

Humans Aren't the Only Ones Who Wear Hats

Remember that all your prospective business hats don't need to be worn by people; some hats can be worn by computers. For example, instead of having an assistant or bookkeeper do your reimbursements for you, download one of the many mobile apps that will keep everything clearly organized by just snapping a photo of your receipt. Instead of wasting time listening to your voicemail, use one of the many apps to transcribe them so you can quickly scan your messages. An app like Otter can record and transcribe your conversations rather than having a human in a meeting there to take notes. The world we live in now is so amazing because we have access to powerful and affordable tools that simplify many business processes. In the "Apply the principles" section of this chapter, there is a link to our favorite business apps to reduce work and simplify your life.

Your Brain Has Room for Only One Hat at a Time

Neuroscience shows that humans are particularly bad at multitasking, but good at convincing ourselves that we're not. Consider what some of the research has to say on the topic:

- Our brains just aren't built for multitasking.[10]

- Multitasking can only work if one of the tasks is automatic (no focus or thought is necessary), and the tasks involve different types of brain processing (like reading while listening to classical music).[11]

- You lose the ability to pay attention to what's going on around you when you multitask.[12]

- Multitasking impairs your cognitive ability similarly to drunkenness (especially if you're behind the wheel).[13]

- Multitasking can create feelings of inadequacy and reduced concentration, which adds more stress.[14]

- Multitasking can come at a cost of 40 percent of your productivity.[15]

- Regular multi-taskers are actually quite bad at it.[16]

As you can see, the science behind wearing more than one hat means embracing the myth of multitasking (there's even a book by that title by Dave Crenshaw). Climbing the mountain is hard enough, so it's important to engineer every advantage you can. The single most important hat to wear is that of "leader," something we'll go into detail with in Pitfall 8: Not Stepping Up as Leader.

---

10 Vidal, R. (2017, April 20). Multitasking Doesn't Work. Retrieved August 24, 2020, from www.huffpost.com/entry/multitasking-doesnt-work_b_9721508.

11 Taylor, J. (2011, March 30). Technology: Myth of Multitasking. Retrieved August 24, 2020, from www.psychologytoday.com/us/blog/the-power-prime/201103/technology-myth-multitasking.

12 Mautz, S. (2017, May 11). Psychology and Neuroscience Blow-Up the Myth of Effective Multitasking. Retrieved August 24, 2020, from www.inc.com/scott-mautz/psychology-and-neuroscience-blow-up-the-myth-of-effective-multitasking.html.

13 Medina, J. (2014). Brain rules: 12 principles for surviving and thriving at work, home, and school. Seattle, WA: Pear Press.

14 Featured Psychology · August 22, 2., Featured Neurology Pain Psychology August 22, 2., Featured Open Neuroscience Articles Psychology August 21, 2., Featured Neuroscience April 28, 2., Also, S., & Featured Genetics Neurology August 12, 2. (2017, April 28). Multitasking Overloads the Brain. Retrieved August 24, 2020, from neurosciencenews.com/multitasking-brain-overload-6531.

15 The True Cost of Multi-Tasking. (2012, September 18). Retrieved August 24, 2020, from www.psychologytoday.com/us/blog/brain-wise/201209/the-true-cost-multi-tasking.

16 Crenshaw, D. (2010, August 20). Is multi-tasking a myth? Retrieved August 24, 2020, from www.bbc.com/news/magazine-11035055.

The purpose of a chapter about wearing different hats is to get you focused on the responsibilities that are solely yours, such as setting the vision, defining the strategy, systematizing the business, clearing obstacles from the path of success, inspiring others, providing leadership, and fostering innovation. Eliminate all other work, stress, and distraction from your life by resisting the impulse to wear all the hats. Legal, accounting, and other minor but important tasks are distractions and will take away from your productivity. They'll also chip away at your peace of mind over time. When I tried keeping my own books and writing my own contracts, there was a persistent and nagging doubt in the back of my mind that the finances were done correctly or my contracts were sound. Having that voice whispering in your ear, "Get ready, because legal consequences are coming our way!" is truly a mental and physical drain. Instead, focus on the responsibilities of the entrepreneur/CEO. Hand all the other hats to those with the training, time, and capability to free you from both the burden and consequences of doing everything but doing it poorly.

Overcoming Pitfall 6: Hand Out the Hats

- Hire an accountant, even if on a part-time basis. If you need help with this, go to the website and do a search for accountants in your area. EntrepreneursParadox.com/Hats.

- Hire a lawyer. If you don't already know one, seek out references from others or search online and find one that looks like a good fit.

- Find an assistant or assistant service.

- If you have employees, hire an outsourced HR company.

- Go to the website to find the most up-to-date business apps that will simplify your life. EntrepreneursParadox.com/Apps.

Pitfall 7

Traveling Alone

"If you want to go fast, go alone. If you want to go far, go together."

—AFRICAN PROVERB

You've likely heard the saying, "It's lonely at the top." This phrase has commonly come to mean that no one understands what the entrepreneur or CEO goes through in order to make the "tough decisions" that lead to success. But it doesn't have to be this way. This chapter will explore how to take the journey up your mountain without the isolation many go through in building a business.

It is true that a lot of entrepreneurs feel lonely when they reach the top of their mountain. Much of this has to do with imposter syndrome as the fear of being exposed as an imperfect, non-genius, non-superhero who somehow "made it" worms its way into the psyche. The truth is, the entrepreneur simply needs an indefatigable drive to execute on an unrelenting vision to succeed. No superhero needed. Like we discussed in the last chapter, it's okay to make mistakes. Lots of them, even, as long as we use each mistake as an opportunity to learn and grow. Once the entrepreneur can accept their own humanness (which includes having empathy and compassion for themselves), they can move forward and make the conscious decision not to isolate. That means shrugging off the imposter syndrome fears and being willing to reach out for help. Everyone already knows you're human, so turning to others isn't going to burst any bubbles. The simple truth is you are not going to be able to achieve your goals by yourself. You will need a support system and key people around you. Even a novelist, one of the most solo-ish careers around, can't do it alone. They need an editor by their side, at the very least. And most successful authors have an agent, a publisher, an illustrator, copy editors, lawyers, PR specialists, and more, all working with and on their behalf. For the entrepreneur, there are three groups of travelers you will need to make it to the top of the mountain. Just like my recent trip up Kilimanjaro, there were fellow travelers, porters, and guides all supporting me up the mountain. For the entrepreneur, this equates to having other entrepreneurs, team members, and coaches or mentors working with you on your ascent. Now, you might think, *I understand the need to have a guide and porter, but fellow travelers...?* So, let's start with that group first.

Find Fellow Travelers (Other Entrepreneurs)

Kilimanjaro is the largest freestanding mountain in the world, and as I made my ascent, it was the final push that was the hardest. Up until summit day, the trek had been fairly easy: we would hike between five and seven miles per day and rose from 6,046 feet to 15,430 feet when we arrived at base camp. We prepared our beds and ate a slightly undercooked meal before going to bed at ten o'clock and waking up at midnight to start hiking again at one o'clock in the morning. From base camp to the top is 3.1 miles and a climb of just under four thousand feet (most of that elevation being in the first two miles). To say it was hard is an understatement. To say it was excruciating is more accurate.

Nearly every step up the final ascent required a deeply inhaled breath
and purposeful movement as we trudged up the skree. We made it
to a small cave where Simon, our main guide, announced we could
rest for five minutes. Every second ticked by like Big Ben's bell in our
heads as they pounded from the effort and high altitude. When Simon
said it was time to go again, I heard someone call out, "Just five more
minutes," like a high schooler not wanting to wake up for school.
The exhaustion and early signs of oxygen deprivation required every
ounce of energy we had just to stand back up. Many in our group
were even considering turning around.

Then a handful of other travelers said, "You flew all the way to Africa
to climb this mountain and you are not giving up now. We are
halfway up the final push to the summit, so get up and keep hiking.
You can do this." Several people shared electrolyte gummies and
other energy-producing snacks and continued to uplift (and in some
cases literally lift) the downtrodden in body and spirit. Through
much encouragement and support, our entire group left the safety
of the cave and continued one step in front of the other to the chants
of *po-le po-le*, up the mountain. Everyone reached the first point at
Gillman's Peak, and again some wanted to head back down. But with
the continued support of the group taking the climb together up
to the "Roof of Africa," everyone made it to the second peak, Stella
Point. From there, all but two made it to the final summit, Uhuru
Peak. Others literally walked arm-in-arm with other expeditioners to
get to the top.

Just like on the mountain, entrepreneurs need a support group that
is climbing with them. Take the journey with others who can bolster
you when you feel like turning around and benefit from your help
as well. And you don't need to ascend to an icy cave on top of the
world to find worthy compatriots; join a professional group such as
Entrepreneurs' Organization, Chamber of Commerce, 10,000 Small
Businesses, an incubator, or other cohort-driven organizations.

Search the local news for startups that are succeeding and ask the founder to lunch. Find out who is winning business awards and set an appointment to meet the founder, tour the office, and hear how the company got started. Once you have two to four peers that you know and trust, form a support group to help each other when the figurative night gets dark and cold and it's hard to breathe. Entrepreneurs' Organization is an organization that does exactly that and is one of the easiest ways to meet others traveling along a similar entrepreneurial journey.

Hire Porters (Team Members)

This will depend on which mountain range you are climbing. If you are climbing a real-world mountain like Timpanogos, you can carry everything you need in a day pack and continue to make the trip yourself daily. You can hike with friends or by yourself. Each night, you return to the comfort and safety of your home. If you want to be a solopreneur, you will not necessarily need employees to help you on your way. If you are going to climb Kilimanjaro or any larger mountain, you will need a team. Hire the best people.

Hiring is one of the most important things you can do in your business. Jim Collins calls it "getting the right people on the bus." If there is one thing that will accelerate or degrade your business faster than any other factor, it's who you hire. Hire first for loyalty, dedication, and attitude. Simon Sinek famously quips, "You don't hire for skills, you hire for attitude. You can always teach skills." Find people who love the journey as much as the destination. Find those who are willing to weather the storm, push through the clouds, and do whatever it takes to make it to the top of the mountain. The two worst hires I ever made were people who, on paper, were the Michael Jordans of the business world. They drove the fancy cars and had a

silver tongue and a pedigree of the top companies a mile long. One of
the best people I hired was an intern with no experience who wanted
to be part of something great and believed in a dream. He was willing
to work late nights and sacrifice because he saw the vision. I've been
really blessed to have worked with so many people just like this.
Don't be starstruck by a big resume full of big businesses. Often this
is the exact wrong fit because they only know how to work in a large
corporate environment and don't understand the start-up world.

Enlist a Guide (Coach or Mentor)

I certainly didn't climb to the top of Kilimanjaro alone. My expedition
included guides and porters in addition to my band of climbing peers.
The man who owned the operation in Africa was named Abdul, and
he served as our main guide. In addition, the Tanzanian government
mandated that each person have one guide and a couple of porters.
The guides were required for safety reasons, and mine was named
Lucas. While it was my first attempt to summit Kilimanjaro, Lucas
had made it to the top over three hundred times; Abdul over five
hundred times. They really knew what they were doing. They had
experience climbing the mountain in rain, snow, and severe heat,
knew what plants to look for on the way up, and which paths to avoid
so we didn't run into predators. They also knew what to wear, how to
fuel the body to have enough energy, and how to spot hypoxia. They
knew when to start different parts of the journey and when it wasn't
safe to move ahead.

I was so grateful to have a guide with me because without Abdul I
wouldn't be here today writing this book. When I reached the final
summit at 19,341 feet, the altitude sickness hit me like a brick wall. I
had become so exhilarated and jubilant upon reaching my goal that I

used much more oxygen than was healthy. My breathing went from hard deep breaths to feeling like I was suffocating. I was so excited to get to the top I didn't anticipate how hard the climb back down would be, especially with constricted airways. Returning to base camp was one of the most excruciating things I have done. Descending the four thousand feet, in and of itself, was hard enough. But dropping that many feet while sipping air through a straw was almost unbearable. When I made it to base camp, Abdul said to rest for an hour and then we would continue down to the next camp…another six miles down the mountain. I crawled into my sleeping bag and for an hour I faded in and out of sleep between violent shaking and coughing fits so harsh I was tasting blood. Abdul came in sixty minutes later and said it was time to start hiking. I was so exhausted from the descent and even more exhausted from the continual shaking, I pleaded with him for another hour of rest. He saw my condition and with very slow and deliberate words looked me straight in the eyes and said, "No. We need to go now!"

I fell out of my sleeping bag and started to change clothes to get ready for another excruciating hike. The trip was painful, and I drifted in and out of wakefulness, at one point dreaming as my body walked me back down the mountain. Four miles later, I felt my lungs expand as suddenly I could breathe! Even though my blood oxygen level was still dangerously low, it was much better than the 81 percent at base camp. I immediately fell into my bunk upon reaching the next camp and slept soundly for a glorious six hours.

When I awoke, Abdul was there and shared how glad he was to see me make it back down. I asked him why he was so happy, and he said solemnly, "If you had stayed, you would have died." This shocked me. Without Abdul, I would have done exactly what I do anytime I get sick—just kept sleeping. Following my tried-and-true recovery routine in an oxygen-deprived environment would have killed me.

Just like Abdul, entrepreneurial guides help keep us safe. They can recognize danger, keep us on the best path, and help us achieve our goals. Such a business guide can be a mentor or coach. I am always impressed by how many people who have successfully climbed the business mountain are ready and willing to help others climb. Think of someone you look up to in the business world. Call them and let them know you are looking for advice on how to achieve great things with your business. Take them to lunch and ask them to be your mentor. One way to accomplish this is to form a board. Start with an advisory board, and as things continue to grow, you can morph that into a board of directors.

Getting a mentor to function as your guide isn't just a nice thought; it is backed by research. 70 percent of businesses where the founder has a consistent mentor survive and thrive for more than five years.[17] This is more than double the success rate of non-mentored startups. Along with that, "93 percent of small business owners agree that mentors have a direct impact on the growth and survival of their business."[18]

Mentors and coaches help companies succeed because they can:

- Offer you accountability

- Motivate you

- Provide unbiased views

- Find weaknesses in your business plan

- Expand your network

- Help you learn critical concepts as an entrepreneur

- Prevent you from making fatal mistakes

- Assist in finding capital if needed

---

17   Rampton, J. (2015, May 21). How a Mentor Can Increase the Success of Your Business. Retrieved September 09, 2020, from www.inc.com/john-rampton/how-a-mentor-can-increase-the-success-of-your-business.html.

18   Gunjahalli, R. (2020, March 13). Five Reasons Why Every Entrepreneur Needs A Great Mentor. Retrieved September 09, 2020, from www.entrepreneur.com/article/347638.

- Offer you a sounding board for difficult problems

- Walk you through growth strategies

- Offer start-up assistance

- Help ensure your first-year success

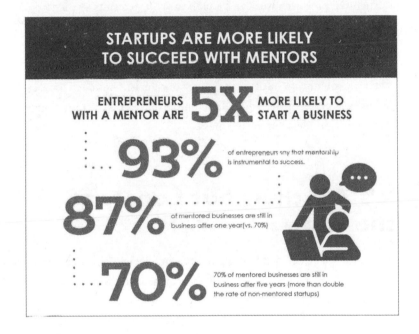

Finding a mentor who will meet regularly can sometimes be a challenge. While advisory boards usually convene once a quarter, I suggest meeting with your mentor more often. If you can't find a mentor who is willing to meet weekly, I would suggest finding a coach. This person can fill the place of a mentor or function with them as part of your team.

Mentor Versus Coach

A coach is different from a mentor, as coaches are focused on accountability and achieving milestones that drive the company to the end destination. Whereas a mentor is someone you can call on occasion when you have questions or concerns, a coach usually has a structured time each week and a plan to achieve results. A mentor often has specific industry-related experience, whereas a coach doesn't need this to help the entrepreneur achieve specific goals. A mentor is usually a lifelong friend through the process, whereas a coach sticks with you until you achieve your goals. The coach focuses on business performance while the mentor focuses on the individual and specific problems in the business.

It's Anything but Lonely at the Top

Hopefully you've decided that the top doesn't have to be lonely. In fact, just like my climb to the top of Kilimanjaro, you're much more likely to succeed if you ascend arm-in-arm with those you've come to trust and rely on. According to Kabbage.com, 61 percent of business owners mentor others. So much for the myth of a mountain full of solo climbers. So get out there and find someone who has blazed the trail ahead of you. And if possible, never eat alone; spend every possible lunch hour with someone who has been where you want to be. This one act alone doubles your chance for success. And who wouldn't want to celebrate "planting the flag" with those who made the journey with you?

Overcoming Pitfall 7: Travel with Friends

- Make a list of millionaires and business owners you know or you would like to know and take one out for lunch every week for the next two months. Ask them questions like:

    - What is their start-up story?

    - What was the most difficult situation they experienced? How did they overcome it?

    - When was a time they failed at something? How did they move past the failure logistically and emotionally?

    - What was the thing they lacked most when starting their first business?

    - Why did they start their first business?

    - Who do they wish they had hired faster? Who do they regret hiring and why?

    - How do they balance work and home life?

    - What piece of advice did they have from a mentor that changed their business or their life?

    - If they could rewind time, what would they do differently?

    - What drives them to get out of bed every morning?

    - How do they keep from getting comfortable? How do they stay motivated to grow and progress?

    - Who was their inspiration when they started their first business, and why?

    - What book are they currently reading?

    - What book is the most important for an entrepreneur?

- Go to the website EntrepreneursParadox.com/Network and find like-minded entrepreneurs and groups in your area. Here is a sample:

- Entrepreneurs' Organizations. EO is a high-quality support network of 14,000+ like-minded leaders across sixty-one countries. They help entrepreneurs achieve their full potential through the power of life-enhancing connections, shared experiences, and collaborative learning.

- Chamber of Commerce. The US Chamber of Commerce is the world's largest business organization, representing companies of all sizes across every sector of the economy and advocating pro-business policies in Washington, DC.

- 10,000 Small Businesses—Goldman Sachs. 10,000 Small Businesses is an investment organization to help entrepreneurs create jobs and economic opportunity by providing access to education, capital, and business support services.

- SCORE. SCORE is the nation's largest network of volunteer, expert business mentors, and is dedicated to helping small businesses get off the ground, grow, and achieve their goals.

- Young President's Organization. YPO is the global leadership community of extraordinary chief executives—more than 29,000 members from 142 countries. Together, executives become better leaders and better people.

- SBDCs. America's SBDC represents America's nationwide network of Small Business Development Center (SBDCs), the most comprehensive small business assistance network in the United States and its territories.

- MBDA Business Centers. The US Department of Commerce Minority Business Development Agency (MBDA) is the only federal agency solely dedicated to the growth and global competitiveness of minority business enterprises.

- Veterans Business Outreach Center. The Veterans Business Outreach Center (VBOC) program is designed to provide entrepreneurial development services such as business training, counseling, and resource partner referrals to transitioning service members, veterans, National Guard and Reserve members, and military spouses interested in starting or growing a small business.

- The Association of Women's Business Centers (AWBC). The AWBC works to secure economic justice and entrepreneurial opportunities for women by supporting and sustaining a national network of more than a hundred Women's Business Centers (WBC). WBCs help women succeed in business by providing training, mentoring, business development, and financing opportunities to over 150,000 women entrepreneurs each year.

- BNI. The mission of BNI is to help members increase their business through a structured, positive, and professional referral marketing program that enables them to develop long-term, meaningful relationships with quality business professionals.

• Create a habit by setting up a rotating weekly call with one of the four entrepreneur peers you trust. With four peers, you will be setting up a call with each only once a month, but will cover four weeks of the month. On the call, brainstorm ways to overcome your most pressing problem of the week. Ask them what they are doing to solve the issue or if they know anyone that has gone through a similar experience you can reach out to.

- Hire a coach or get a mentor.

Pitfall 8

Not Stepping Up
as a Leader

Leadership is a verb, not a noun: an action not a title.

Leadership is a constant learning experience. It is not something that one can become, but rather is something one is always becoming. As your team expands, your leadership will have to expand. As the company grows, you will have to grow as a leader. As your markets expand to other locations and even globally, your leadership skills will have to expand. Leadership is about continuously becoming. This chapter will set some guidelines to help with your "becoming."

You've wrestled alligators, pulled the drain plug on the swamp, picked your mountain, formed a team, found a guide, and overcome your fears to take your business to the next level. Now you're facing more than a few eager faces waiting for you to lead them—to point the way to the top of the mountain and then lead the way. So how do you go from alligator wrestler to leader? This is one of the biggest leaps in rewriting your story and jumping from start-up founder to true entrepreneur. Accepting the call to become the leader is an inflection point in all startups as the realization hits home that you require more than a technician to make this company succeed; you need someone out front directing the way forward. Once the realization hits that this company has grown to the point where it needs a leader, there are only three directions to go:

1. Step Up… Take the bull by the horns and step up as the leader. You've accepted the challenge to do whatever it takes to make your company succeed.

2. Step Back… Scale the business back down. If the mantle of leadership seems overwhelming, you can always choose to go back to being the technician in your garage/basement/kitchen and not worry about growing. You've accepted being a solopreneur, poised to handle everything yourself as long as this doesn't get too big.

3. Step to the Side… Hire someone else to lead.

The benefits of scaling the business down are:

- There is a perception of less stress.

- You know that, as long as you only have a handful of clients, you can get things done the way you want them and with the quality you know you can produce.

- You don't have to change who you are right now.

- It's comfortable and much easier than transforming into someone new.

The drawbacks of scaling the business down are:

- Less revenue

- Fewer profits

- Not as much excitement

- Less purpose

- More hats to wear (once again)

Stepping up as the leader has these benefits:

- It's exciting.

- It's purpose-driven.

- It opens new frontiers.

- You get to reinvent yourself.

- You can achieve more revenue.

- You can achieve amazing things.

- You have a chance to change the world.

- You can achieve more revenue.

- You experience more financial freedom.

These are the things that can make stepping up as the leader challenging:

- More excitement can mean more stress. It doesn't have to, but it can.

- It takes work; it is outside of the comfort zone.

- You will have to find a new passion around building the business instead of the product or service.

- You will have to work with people. Lots of people.

- You will have to trust others at a level you have never trusted before; you'll be handing your "baby" over to the care of others.

- You'll have to understand finances and KPIs with the same level of passion and drive that you know your product.

The challenges and risks in hiring a leader almost always outweigh any potential benefits, and this is the choice I've seen go astray the most. Typically, the entrepreneur loses his passion as the new leader changes the direction of the company. It almost always happens that a new leader will have a different vision and will often choose a different path. Disheartened, the entrepreneur ends up leaving within six months to a year (and it's rarely amicable). I suggest staying away from this choice.

When the inflection point of stepping up to be the leader came in my first business, I did a Google search for, "What does a CEO do?" The answers weren't very helpful, and I didn't know how to utilize the information I was reading. I didn't know how or why I was going to lead a board of directors. A better search would have been, "How can I become a great leader?" or "What makes great leaders?"

THE **BEST LEADERS** AREN'T CONCERNED
about
WHO'S RIGHT OR **WHAT'S RIGHT**
simply
WHAT'S BEST

Now you might push back and say, "Hey Curtis, so I don't need to worry about what's 'right?' Doesn't what's right equal what's moral?" No. When a leader does what's "best," that encompasses what's right while decoupling the idea from any personal agendas. Different religions, societies, governments, organizations, and groups have different versions of what's "right." In this definition of best, it always includes what's moral, upright, legal, and ethical. The big difference— no agendas. No one marks a line in the sand. All perspectives and ideas are valued on their own merits.

The Six Jobs of an Entrepreneurial Leader

There are six jobs for the entrepreneurial leader of a start-up.

1. Set the Vision—See the top of the mountain and uncover the epic adventure.

2. Inspire Others—Help those around you believe in themselves and their ability to contribute to this epic journey.

3. Clear the Path for Success and Systematize Your Business— Take the decision-making out of the business. Extract the "Secret Sauce" and make it replicable.

4. Lead—Take the first step. Lead by example. Allow others to make mistakes and be willing to make them yourself.

5. Foster Innovation—Create a culture of innovation. Create a company that thinks outside the box.

6. Be 100 Percent Accountable—Own your actions for better or worse. Own your failures and victories. Create your future and the future of your company.

Job One: See the Top of the Mountain and Uncover the Epic Adventure

There's a reason I listed this first—everything else along your entrepreneurial journey is dependent on this step. As humans, we yearn for adventure; we need purpose. Take a look at this simple yet daunting ad listed in a British newspaper called *The Times* in 1900: "Men wanted for hazardous journey, small wages, bitter cold, long months of complete darkness, constant danger, safe return doubtful, honor and recognition in case of success."

waste   ur time unless thoroughly
qualified. Mr. L. Barker 1408 Chap-
man Bldg.

MEN WANTED

for hazardous journey, small wages,
bitter cold, long months of complete
darkness, constant danger, safe return doubtful, honor and recognition
in case of sucess.

Ernest Shackleton 4 Burlington st.

MEN—Neat-appearing young men of
pleasing personality, between the ages
of 21 to 40 to work at leath

Without the last line, this ad would have no appeal—it would seem ridiculous. Adding the last line, "…honor and recognition in event of success" changed the ad from something absurd to something inspiring. Without literally saying it, Sir Ernest Shackleton conveyed, *we will achieve great things on this expedition.* Five thousand men applied to be part of the first expedition to cross the "South polar continent from sea to sea." Can you imagine applying for a job with guaranteed "low wages" and "long months of complete darkness?" Or, even more audacious, can you imagine sending an email today with that kind of job offer? My last business partner did exactly that. He painted a brilliant vision of contribution and stated very clearly up front, "this will not be the highest paying job you can get. In fact, you are worth much more than we can pay you." People worked for eLearning Brothers not because of pay. Seven top-level employees gave up their own ventures to join the company because they believed in the vision of greatness painted by Andrew Scivally, and they believed they could contribute in a significant way to that vision.

Sir Ernest Shackleton understood how to inspire people with a sense of purpose, adventure, and vision. He was able to tap into that very human yearning to find adventure, to find greatness. We humans need a quest in life; so much so that "purpose" is the number-one indicator of longevity.

Some of the greatest entrepreneurs in our recent past include Steve Jobs, Elon Musk, and Jeff Bezos. Each of these leaders resisted starting with "What" then moving on to "How" and "Why." True leaders start with "Why," then figure out the "How," which leads to the "What." Elon said, "We need to be an interplanetary race by inhabiting Mars so our species can survive a catastrophe if one ever happens on earth." That's the Why. He created Tesla because extraterrestrial vehicles needed to be electric, and that's the only guaranteed energy source on Mars. He started SpaceX because we need a way to get there. He asked his cousins Peter and Lyndon Rive to create SolarCity and then bought their company so he could harness the sun's energy when humans begin to settle the red planet.

Job Two: Inspire Others to Believe in Themselves and Their Ability to Contribute to This Epic Journey

Elon Musk started with an INSPIRING vision that drew people to him and made the journey up the mountain feel possible. Like Bilbo Baggins in *The Hobbit*, we all have to believe the journey is worth leaving the safety of the Shire. Such commitment is the responsibility of the leader to bring to life.

Stephen Covey said, "Leadership is communicating others' worth and potential so clearly that they are inspired to see it in themselves." One of the greatest jobs of a leader is to create a specific path for each person to engage in and contribute to. As an entrepreneur, this means you need to hire every member of your direct team yourself; do not abdicate this role. Until you know that each person has the same innate fervor for the mission you're embarking on, keep hiring every person yourself. Hire every person yourself until you have created leaders out of those you've hired; that way you'll know they'll follow the same pattern when it is their turn to create the next line of leaders as they actively create a culture of ownership and excitement.

Job Three: Clear the Path for Success

As a leader, it is your job to create systems and processes that increase the speed and likelihood of success. If someone falls short, it's more likely the system around that person that failed, rather than the person themself. Successful leaders understand that when they focus on the success of their people, the company's success will follow. Your job is to clear the path for individual success and systemic success by ensuring people know how they can contribute and how that contribution connects to the larger success of the company.

When it comes to putting systems in place, your goals are to increase speed, efficiency, consistency, profits, and enjoyment. A great way to think about this is the franchise model. Imagine you're setting up another "shop" and want to ensure the quality and efficiency you've mastered in doing your own work. You'd want to create systems that:

- Perform the same way every time.

- Eliminate human error by reducing the decision-making processes.

Your franchise goal is to create a company that can function even with the least qualified person performing the responsibilities. I often hear the phrase, "Well, we can't do that because our secret sauce is our creativity and that's dependent on [insert name here]." Don't fool yourself; creativity is already a process. You just need to document it and duplicate it.

The next statement I often hear from entrepreneurs is, "Well, then we will lose our best creative minds because they don't want to be robots." This is also a fallacy; if you systematize the creative process, it actually frees people up to be *more* creative. The creative process is just that: a process—it can be documented and duplicated. You'll be surprised how much more you can create and how much more fun you'll have doing it when you eliminate the multiple minute decisions along the way. Do this for every department as if you were creating a manual that your out-of-state franchisee will depend on.

One example many companies struggle with is the sales team. At one company I worked with, they created a multi-tiered sales compensation structure as they went out to hire salespeople. The previous system had only one tier and wasn't as motivating, so the new system seemed like a great idea—the more the salesperson sold, the higher the commission. After a few weeks, the head of sales noticed that the salespeople weren't as effective and the plan seemed to be backfiring. The team was making fewer overall sales and was distracted throughout the day. When the head of sales put on his Sherlock hat and investigated, he found that the salespeople were busy calculating their end-of-month commissions and pay structure after every sale. All that time spent calculating instead of selling was actually hampering their performance! In this case, it was the system itself that was flawed and getting in the way. As soon as this was discovered, the owner and head of sales amended the system by creating a shared Google Doc (they weren't quite large enough to invest in Salesforce yet) that automatically calculated the commissions. As soon as the salesperson logged the sale, they knew exactly what to expect on their next payroll check. This simple new system worked well, and the process could be duplicated and shared. As the team and their success grew, they eventually moved to Salesforce and implemented a new system that more fully met their needs.

Job Four: Lead by Example and Take the First Step

John Quincy Adams said, "If your actions inspire others to dream more, learn more, do more, and become more, you are a leader." Never ask someone to do something you're unwilling to do yourself. You took the first steps in creating your product, company, and expanding it beyond yourself. Continue to set the example of a high work ethic, culture, vision, positivity, and adaptability to changing market conditions. Every person in the company looks to your example more than your words when it comes to guiding their daily actions. When things get really rough, set the example again by drawing on your mentor and other entrepreneurs you've surrounded yourself with for strength. Show those on your team that it's okay to be vulnerable, honest, and accountable to yourself and those on your team. If you don't trust yourself as a leader capable of doing these things, set up a regular call with your mentor for advice, or even hire a counselor or coach. The fact that you created a company clearly shows that you are strong—now turn that strength toward new and better leadership practices.

Job Five: Foster Innovation

The more enjoyable the work environment, the better the employee retention and the higher the quality of work. This is true in any organization. One of the ways to create that environment is by fostering innovation.

People love to solve challenges. It is built into our DNA. Our human nature leans toward innovation. We want to create. We want to make things better, bigger, smaller, faster, lighter, and stronger.

Your job as a leader is to make sure that the company you build has a culture of innovation. Bake creative problem solving right into every workday. There are several ways to do this. The famed example of Google setting aside 20 percent of an employee's workweek has resulted in the creation of some of the most significant products for the company including Gmail, Google News, and even Ad Sense (one of the top revenue-producing channels for the multi-billion-dollar company. Another company created an "Idea Box."

People would submit ideas into the Idea Box, and every week the leadership would draw out the best idea and publicly award the person with fifty dollars in the company meeting.

Bake it into your culture and also exhibit it yourself. For most entrepreneurs, this is not hard. This is where you thrive. Make sure to bring your ideas to the team and be innovative in the product and service features but also be innovative in building the company. Be innovative in how the company is managed. Be innovative in how you work with clients. Be innovative in all aspects of your business.

Job Six: Own Your Mistakes and Successes

Your last job as a leader is to assume 100 percent responsibility for what happens in your company, including every mistake or misstep. People are much more willing to trust those who acknowledge their weaknesses than those who give excuses or shuck responsibility. I fell into this trap several times myself, taking on the role of "the Expert" in my own imposter syndrome. I thought I always had to have the answers, but what I discovered is that respect comes from sharing the truth, not being able to spin it. If you don't have all the answers, that's okay; admit it.

A word of caution: I have seen many entrepreneurs claim to live by the mantra that any failings of the company are theirs, but any successes are due to everyone else. This isn't true, and people will see through the insincerity of getting up in front of a crowd and claiming you had nothing to do with the success. The truth is that it takes everyone (including you) on the expedition to make it to the top of the mountain. Acknowledge everyone's contributions without deprecating yourself in the process.

Mistakes and missteps are actually blessings to a small business; they are indicators that there are ways for the company to grow. Mistakes are not something to be ashamed of, but rather something to embrace. You are the foundation for the success of the company. Own every part of it.

Overcoming Pitfall 8: Become the Leader

- Add in "ship" to "leader" like so: Go to the website EntrepreneursParadox.com/LeaderSurvey and take the leadership assessment.

- Ask yourself a very hard question, "Is there anything I have currently asked others to do that I am not willing to do or haven't done myself?"

    - Showing up at work early.

    - Working longer hours.

- Doing difficult tasks.

- Having hard conversations.

- What is one process that, if systematized, would have the greatest impact on the company today?

- What is your vision for where the company can go? Ask yourself, "Is it inspiring?" If not, find a passion in your purpose.

- Write down every person in your direct team and list one way you can help them become a leader in your organization.

Pitfall 9

Entrepreneurial Neglect

Caring for yourself is the most important thing you can do in contributing to the world. You are the only permanent caretaker of your body, mind, and soul. Giving the world a healthy you is giving a divine gift.

The most valuable asset in the company is you; it's not your product, your people, your capital, or your brand. Imagine climbing the big mountain with a broken leg—you could possibly do it, but it would be painful and cause more damage the further you go. Protecting the asset means watching out for yourself, but a lack of self-care is a chronic problem with entrepreneurs. Why? We tend to neglect ourselves and sacrifice our health, family, sleep, and sometimes even personal wealth for the good of the company. And without you driving your vision forward, the company will stumble or veer off course completely. The best asset we have for making a contribution to the world is ourselves. If we underinvest in ourselves, and by that I mean our minds, our bodies, and our spirits, we damage the very tool we need to make our highest contribution. So, don't be afraid to take care of yourself; it's actually one of the most important things you can do for the company. Remember, burning the candle at both ends quickly leaves you without light.

In the book *Essentialism: The Disciplined Pursuit of Less* by Greg
McKeown, there's an entire section on the concept of protecting
the asset, and I recommend reading it if you want to go deeper
into this topic. For now, I'll share the most common ways I've seen
entrepreneurs neglect themselves; I'll provide solutions for each and
propose a formula for maintaining and improving your whole person
called the Power Hour. Please keep in mind, however, that I'm not a
doctor, nutritionist, or exercise physiologist. Please construe nothing
in this chapter as medical advice. Always consult with your doctor
before beginning an exercise, sleep, or nutritional program.

One last word of caution: I have a fairly regimented routine that
I follow both morning and night. This chapter isn't meant to be a
line-by-line prescription that you need to follow. By sharing what
works for me, I hope you focus on the spirit of the message and not
the letter. What you find invigorating, renewing, and energizing may
differ from what works for me. Likewise, the amount of time you have
available, the hours that you keep, your personal circadian rhythm,
will all be unique to you. The point is to do something and then build
from there.

Sleep

Not needing sleep has seemingly become a badge of honor in the
entrepreneurial community. I don't know where this mindset
originated, but I bought into it for a long time. Sleep deprivation
seems to be the most common form of entrepreneurial neglect. The
damage it causes is also one of the most underestimated. According
to the CDC,[19] sleep deprivation creates "cognitive impairment" equal
to being legally drunk: "Being awake for at least twenty-four hours is

---

19   CDC—Drowsy Driving—Sleep and Sleep Disorders. (2017, March 21). Retrieved September 12, 2020, from
      www.cdc.gov/sleep/about_sleep/drowsy_driving.html.

equal to having a blood alcohol content of 0.10 percent. This is higher than the legal limit (0.08 percent BAC) in all states."

Staying up late to work on projects can seem like the right decision, but it's actually counterproductive. The longer a person stays awake, the lower and slower the cognitive functioning. It's a self-perpetuating problem—the longer you stay awake, the less productive you become. This means staying up later to get your work done perpetuates the declining cycle. Go to bed when you're feeling the stupor set in. If there is a critical deadline, wake up early when you can be at full capacity, instead of staying up late. It's not just about being productive. Harvard researcher Christoph Randler found early risers to be more proactive, more apt in anticipating problems, and more efficient at minimizing issues.[20] A University of Toronto study reported that morning people experience a higher degree of happiness.[21] These factors lead to greater success in and out of the business world. So get the sleep you need; if you have to sacrifice some of it to meet a deadline, do it in the morning by waking up early.

Arianna Huffington is one of the most outspoken advocates for the "Sleep Revolution" and has written a book by the same name. It took fainting and breaking her cheekbone on her desk for her to answer the "wake-up call." Get in touch with your circadian rhythm and recognize adults typically need seven to eight hours of sleep a night.[22] Wouldn't you like to be more refreshed and ready to face the challenges ahead of you rather than trudge through the day?

Here are some guidelines to get the most restful and peaceful night's sleep.

---

20   Randler, C. (2009, December 09). Proactive People Are Morning People1. Retrieved September 12, 2020, from onlinelibrary.wiley.com/doi/abs/10.1111/j.1559-1816.2009.00549.x.

21   Early to bed, early to rise? (n.d.). Retrieved September 12, 2020, from www.utoronto.ca/news/early-bed-early-rise.

22   Pinker, S. (2018, October 25). When It Comes to Sleep, One Size Fits All. Retrieved September 12, 2020, from www.wsj.com/articles/when-it-comes-to-sleep-one-size-fits-all-1540481975.

Bright light during the day and no blue light at night. To sleep the most restfully, follow the natural pattern of the sun. During the day, expose yourself to natural sunlight and make sure to turn off blue light at night. It's not just about getting rid of blue light. It is actually more beneficial for your circadian rhythm to be exposed to bright light during the day. The brighter the light and longer you are exposed to daylight, the better you sleep at night. Although we think of the sun as a glowing yellow ball in the sky, if you look at where it sits on the color spectrum, the sun is the number one source of blue light. Ask any well-trained photographer, and they can tell you daylight is in the range of 5,900K to 8,000 K (kelvin)—this means blue. At night, the sun sets beneath the horizon and the temperatures shift to the warm colors around 3,900 K. Your brain needs those warmer colors to tell it to wind down and get ready for a good night's sleep. Blue light at night disrupts this indicator. The number one source of blue light at night is electronics. Give yourself a minimum of thirty minutes (preferably two hours) before bed without looking at a screen of any kind. If your home has smart lights, set them for daylight between six o'clock in the morning and eight o'clock at night, and then set them to the warmer colors at night.

Train your sleep brain.

- Create a consistent pre-sleep routine. One of the brain's superpowers is pattern recognition. Create a pattern that your brain can identify that will start the shut-down process. Put on your pajamas after a hot bath or shower. Then, sip on a nice cup of chamomile tea while reading a physical (non-digital) book. Next, brush your teeth and say your prayers or meditate. Then, hop into bed. Whatever your routine, whatever you find most relaxing, create a consistent pattern you repeat night after night that tells your brain it's time to wind down and prepare to rest.

- Same time every night. Same time every morning. Your circadian rhythms are just that: rhythms. Like the rhythm in a song, it is consistent and regular. Hitting the hay each night at the same time and waking at the same time will train your sleep brain very effectively.

No Long Naps. One of the best ways to disrupt your brain's circadian rhythms is to take naps longer than thirty minutes or nap after two or three o'clock in the afternoon. Shorter naps, of ten to twenty minutes, can produce a significant boost in productivity during the day, especially before two o'clock. People taking longer naps report grogginess and cognitive impairment. Longer naps also trick the body into thinking it is time to sleep and confuse your circadian rhythms.

Create a sleep haven. Here are some quick and easy tips for changing your sleep environment to significantly increase your chances of a restful night.

- Create a cool environment. Set the thermostat to 65–70°F (18–21°C). It's harder to sleep when it's hot. The body naturally cools down while sleeping, which is a way to signal the brain that it's time to sleep.

- Remove devices from your sleep sanctuary. Keep your bed sacrosanct for sleeping. Don't bring work, Facebook, or any other distraction to bed. Your brain becomes alert just knowing your phone is nearby. Give your brain a break and let it rest.

- Give yourself the gift of a comfortable bed and pillow. I'm sure you know the relaxing feeling of collapsing into a comfortable bed and letting sleep overcome you. If you don't feel that in your current bed, it might be time to go shopping. Start with the pillow because it can have as much of an impact on your sleep quality as a new mattress.

- The darker the more restful. Remove or cover any distracting lights in your room. Close the shades (use blackout shades if you can). You can even wear a night mask in locations where you can't get it completely dark. Light signals the brain to wake up. Even small lights can send a disrupting signal to the brain.

You may also consider painting the walls in darker, more soothing colors.

- Reduce the noise. Make your room as quiet as possible. Cover windows, close doors, decorate your room with sound-absorbing material like cloth and sound-dampening panels. If you live in a busy area near traffic or other noises, consider a white noise machine for the bedroom.

Consume the helpful and remove the harmful. What you put in your mouth before bed can either help you sleep or keep your brain wide awake.

The helpful list includes:

- Chamomile tea (noncaffeinated). Chamomile is shown to relax the body and increase sleep patterns similar to a hot bath or shower.

- Magnesium. I love the brand Calm before bed.

- Melatonin. This is the sleep chemical in your brain. If your brain is not producing it well enough, you can add a melatonin supplement to get you into those deep sleep patterns.

- Other natural supplements, like valerian root, ginkgo biloba, glycine, L-theanine, and lavender.

Do not start taking these all at once but experiment with various supplements individually to see which one your body likes the best.

The harmful list consists of:

- Caffeine (especially after two or three in the afternoon). We have become a caffeine-dependent society. If you choose the daily boost, do it before the mid-afternoon or you will stay awake unnecessarily.

- Alcohol. All forms of alcohol are known to increase and even cause symptoms related to snoring, sleep apnea, and disrupted sleep patterns and decrease melatonin production and human growth hormone (HGH).

- Large amounts of water. Save yourself a midnight trip to the bathroom by limiting water one to two hours before bed. Make a trip to the bathroom part of your nighttime routine.

- Food right before bed. This can also prevent the production of HGH and melatonin. Plus, you're more likely to take a trip to the bathroom which will disrupt your sleep.

Protecting the asset means turning your nights from a downward-spiraling, sleep-deprived stupor into one of your greatest advantages of personal productivity. Get the sleep you need, and your body will reward you with clear thinking, a positive attitude, and greater overall healing and health.

Exercise

Exercise is a fantastic way to increase your chances for success. Exercise is a natural stress reliever and antidepressant, and it enhances several areas of the brain at once, including memory. Exercise allows the brain time to defocus and solve problems for you and is a great way to increase your lung capacity and burn calories along the way. One big benefit of regular exercise is that it is a confidence builder. If you are pushing through a marathon, bike race, triathlon, or CrossFit competition, or really pushing yourself to new heights, it will build confidence that will flow over to your everyday life.

On Dec. 26, 1960, President-elect John F. Kennedy penned an article in *Sports Illustrated* called "The Soft American." In it he wrote, "Physical fitness is not only one of the most important keys to a healthy body, it is the basis of dynamic and creative intellectual activity." Science would later find his claim to be true.[23] Exercise not only helps build muscles in the arms and legs but builds intellectual muscle, stamina, and endurance as well. For the mental benefits of exercise, it:

- Pumps more oxygen to the brain

- Releases hormones which provide an excellent environment for the growth of brain cells

- Promotes brain plasticity (the ability of the brain to change and adapt) by stimulating growth of new connections between cells

- Increases the growth factors which make it easier for the brain to grow new neuronal connections (neurogenesis)

- Reduces stress hormones

- Prompts more cell growth in the hippocampus (the area of the brain responsible for learning and memory)

- Shows promise as an antidepressant

- Focuses concentration

- Spurs creativity

- Slows cognitive degradation

You may be thinking, *I'm barely getting everything done as it is right now. How am I going to fit exercise into my day?* The best-case scenario is to get out running, cycling, weightlifting, or swimming for an hour per day. If your calendar doesn't allow for an hour of exercise, see what you can drop from your schedule. Trade TV, social media, or YouTube for exercise. I promise the time is there, the priority is the missing piece. Make taking care of yourself a priority. Along with a regular routine, keep in mind there are ways to multitask exercise and work:

---

23   Armstrong, G. (2018, December 26). How Exercise Affects Your Brain. Retrieved September 11, 2020, from www.scientificamerican.com/article/how-exercise-affects-your-brain.

- **Walking desks**. I've used a walking desk for years and love the mental clarity I get from walking while working. It takes about twenty minutes of walking at a sweat-free pace of two miles per hour before the effect kicks in. At the twenty-minute mark, my scattered thoughts start to become organized. The capacity for greater focus and mental clarity can be achieved simply by walking at a mild pace. I've tried cycling desks as well and found them a little more distracting but still effective.

- **Walking meetings**. Who says meetings need to be in a stuffy conference room? Take your meetings outside; stretch your legs with those you're solving problems with. Find a park, river, trail, or local wilderness area and breathe the fresh air while discussing the issues at hand. You'll be surprised how much more effective such meetings are versus the standard conference room table drudgery. Bring a notepad with you to jot down ideas and action items, or use one of my favorite apps like Otter which transcribes conversations directly into text (and even identifies speakers individually).

- **Walking phone calls**. Never take a call sitting down; stand up and either walk or stretch. You can do it in your office if it is a private call or walk the halls of your building or outside if there is no sensitive information being discussed.

- **Bike or run to work**. If you are close enough to do so, strap on your helmet or running shoes and head to the office. This one does require the office to have a shower—nobody likes a stinky entrepreneur.

- **Make working out a part of your company culture.** This is one of my favorite ways to exercise while building a business. As part of one of my companies, we sponsored a race for everyone in the company from a 5k all the way up to a full marathon. We also sponsored a Ragnar team or two. The effect it had on the company was meaningful—not only did we become a tighter-knit group, but some of the employees took the challenge and lost a significant amount of weight (one person lost over ninety pounds!). It's fun to run as a company and you're able to get to know people on a different level. Be mindful of those with physical limitations or disabilities as you build an exercise culture that is ultimately inclusive, accepting, and available to all.

Diet

Dr. Daniel Amen is one of the leading neuroscientists in the world. He has done more functional magnetic resonance imaging scans on the human brain than anyone on the planet. He describes the effect of eating healthy on the brain and what foods are healthiest:

- Lean protein, such as turkey or chicken.

- Low-glycemic, high-fiber carbohydrates, which means carbohydrates high in fiber that do not raise your blood sugar, such as whole grains and green leafy vegetables.

- Healthy fats that contain omega-three fatty acids, found in foods such as tuna, salmon, avocados, and walnuts.

Since the brain is 85 percent water, anything that dehydrates you is bad for the brain, such as alcohol, caffeine, excess salt, or lack of fluids. Drink plenty of water to keep yourself well-hydrated. By the way, serotonin, the happy neurotransmitter, is produced mostly in the digestive tract. Eating a proper diet of healthy fats and protein like nuts, cheese, and red meat can enhance the production of serotonin.

Mental Health

Breathe; be present. Give yourself a calm place every morning and specifically set aside time to pray, breathe, and meditate. This is a great time to visualize the top of the mountain. In fact, a friend of mine never schedules hour-long meetings, only fifty-minute meetings instead. Then he spends the last ten minutes breathing, reviewing, and preparing.

Family and Social

Give yourself time to be with family and friends so you can rejuvenate. If you are 100 percent business-focused 100 percent of the time, that's not healthy. You need to maintain balance and be there for your family. This is one of my greatest regrets in starting companies: I worked a lot. Even though I was there for every ball game, campout, dance performance, and concert, I would often come home late because I was working on an "important" client project. Family is the most important thing, so spend time with yours and make the most of every second. Don't neglect them, regardless of how important a client is, because you won't be spending the rest of your life with a client. You *will* be spending the rest of your life with your spouse, significant other, and kids. Make every moment count. If you have kids, love them, and squeeze them tight. Put your phone away when you're with them. Tuck them in each night and listen to their hearts—be the parent they need. Look directly into your spouse or significant other's eyes every night and morning and tell them how much you love them. This is where true happiness lies, regardless of how successful your company is.

Financial

The first time I procured investment funds, I was running a multimillion-dollar company and paying myself $50,000 a year. I described to my investors how I led a fairly frugal lifestyle. To my surprise, the investors laughed at that and suggested I pay myself

more. When I replied, "Like $60,000?" they laughed again. I ended
up learning a valuable lesson: the investors wanted me to be paid well
enough that I could eliminate outside financial stressors in my life.
They understood the importance of "protecting the asset." As you
do the same, it's critical that you reduce any unnecessary stressors
from your life so you can show up with your game face on every
day. If you're worrying about your mortgage, you won't be able to
think about your company. Protecting the asset means taking care of
yourself so you can take care of the company.

Fun

Don't forget to enjoy life. Spend each day to the fullest with no regrets
and embrace the adage of "work hard, play hard." When it's time to
play, be present in the moment and let the cares and worries of the
world disappear for an hour or two. Use that time as a way to refresh.
Schedule vacations with your family, and don't be on the phone or
computer when your family needs you at Disneyland or at the beach.
It is hard to disconnect—I get it. I will never forget (and now regret)
the time I was at the Magic Kingdom, sitting on a bench with my
laptop as my family romped around the park without me. Distribute
your responsibilities ahead of time and let your clients know you're
going "off the grid." Plan for emergencies and have someone in
charge and empowered to deal with the unexpected.

Make fun more than just an annual event. Make sure you're enjoying
life daily and weekly too. It can be a game of foosball with team
members, a bike ride, a card game with your family, etc. Letting
yourself relax with enjoyable activities pauses the cortisol (the stress
hormone) production. Too much cortisol over a sustained period of
time leads to anxiety, depression, headaches, chronic stress, weight
gain, sleep problems, and brain function impairment. Replace the

cortisol with endorphins, serotonin, and epinephrine by laughing and playing with those you love.

The Power Hour

So, how do you fit all those fun activities into your life and still have time for work? As promised at the beginning of the chapter, I have come to embrace a formula for doing so. Because the morning is the most productive, proactive, and energizing time of the day, this is a great time to set the rest of the day up for success.

> *"We are what we repeatedly do.*
> *Excellence, then, is not*
> *an act, but a habit."*

Every morning is a new day. It is a brand-new opportunity for you to move closer to the top of the mountain and achieve greatness. Every day is a gift for your benefit. The morning is a time when you can lock in your power for the rest of the day. As we've seen with the research, the morning is a magical opportunity to get your day started right. At first, it may seem mechanical to go down your checklist of items and may take a couple of weeks before it feels natural and revitalizing. So, stick with it and exclude anything urgent from your routine. Remember, this is your time, where you can wake up before the hustle and bustle and make space for yourself and your heart. Give yourself this gift by taking a digital detox: keep the phone off, don't look at emails, and lock in your power for the rest of the day. Here is an example of a morning routine:

- Prayer/meditation

- Exercise (go for a run, swim, or ride)

- Review your daily plan

- Eat a healthy breakfast

- Visualize your mountain in vivid detail

- Recite affirmations audibly

- Start your day with gratitude by writing down three things you're grateful for today

- Write a thank-you card for a team member

Prayer/Meditation

Pray or meditate to get yourself centered first thing in the morning. This will set the tone for the day. There are even apps out there like Headspace or Calm to start the day in a peaceful place.

Go for a Run, Swim, or Ride

Get your blood pumping, muscles moving, and metabolism revved up. You can use this time to listen to an audiobook or a podcast that you've been looking forward to. Use this time as your Zen-time, when you practice being present and conscious.

Review Your Daily Plan

Your daily plan needs to include the top three things that are essential for you to finish that day. Just as important as your "To-do" list is your "To-don't" list and your "To-delegate" list. Mark down the three absolute necessities on your "To-do" list and then add other items you would like to get done but that don't have the same priority. Next, think about the fun activities or distractions and put them on the "To-don't" list. Finally, write down your "To-delegate" list of important things that need to get done but can be accomplished by others.

Mental fatigue is real and the longer the day goes on, the harder it is to accomplish heavy tasks. Put those tasks on the list first. Once you have them organized, close your eyes and visualize yourself completing the top three. If you have difficult tasks in front of you, write out "I am excited" statements about the result of accomplishing the task.

Here is an example to get you started:

TO DO TODAY

MUST DO

1.
2.
3.

HOPE TO DO

1.
2.
3.
4.
5.
6.

TO DON'T TODAY

TO DELEGATE

	Name	Task
1.		
2.		
3.		
4.		
5.		
6.		
7.		
8.		

TO DON'T

MUST DO: Top three most critical action items to move you forward.

HOPE TO DO: Other tasks you would like to get done but aren't top three today.

TO DELEGATE: Tasks you will ask others for their help with.

TO DON'T: Tasks you conciously choose not to do today.

©THE ENTREPRENEUR'S PARADOX

Eat a Healthy Breakfast

Slow-digesting protein, like eggs or an omelet, in the morning lasts longer than empty carbs like cold cereal. Good oatmeal will also provide a more sustained energy release. Have a tasty breakfast and savor it by enjoying the flavors and smells. Soak up the sensory pleasures.

Visualize Your Mountain in Vivid Detail

See yourself succeeding. See yourself achieving the goal. Picture where you are, what clothes you are wearing, who is with you when it happens, and the excitement of those around you (See Pitfall 3: Pulling a Goal Out of Thin Air).

Recite Affirmations Audibly

Create your own affirmations that let you reprogram yourself toward positive self-talk and positive personal imagery, and then say them out loud. Defeat imposter syndrome with positive affirmations. Here are some examples:

- My goals manifest in direct response to my efforts.

- I choose to take complete responsibility for myself and my company.

- I make a difference in the world by providing exceptional products, creating wealth, and providing careers for others.

- I am confident in what I know and recognize that failure is part of the process. Fail fast. My failures and successes do not define me.

- I can learn something from every person I interact with.

- I choose joy over happiness, wealth over money, kindness over niceness, and people over processes.

- I'm willing to have hard conversations when necessary, done in love.

Start Your Day with Gratitude

Write down three things for which you are grateful today. One of the scientifically proven ways to be happy is to express your gratitude and thankfulness for another. Capture these thoughts in a journal and, when appropriate, share them with those you are grateful for.

Write a Thank-You Card for a Team Member

Just after the gratitude exercise is a great time to write a thank-you card for a fellow team member.

Evening Peace Plan

Studies also show nighttime can be the most creative and reflective time, so it is not necessarily a great time to make critical decisions (although individual circadian rhythms can vary). For most, the evening is a great time to enjoy creative hobbies, relax, unwind, and reflect. During this time you can:

- Tuck the kids in bed, spend time with family.

- Review appointments for the next day and turn the cell phone off for the night.

- Journal about your day.

- Engage in a relaxing and creative hobby like guitar or drawing.

- Pray/meditate.

- Leave your phone outside your bedroom and sleep peacefully.

Tuck the Kids in Bed or Spend Time Connecting with a Loved One

Connect with your family. Human connection is vital for life, so make sure you share connections with your kids, spouse, or significant other every day.

Review Appointments for Tomorrow

Review your schedule and make a mental note of what you expect to happen and what you need to prepare for with each calendar item.

Journal About Your Day

This is the key activity for nighttime. Journal truth about your day, viewing it as your personal therapist to get your feelings out, but also to enhance your life. Steep a nice cup of chamomile herbal tea (no caffeine) which aids in restful sleep. Listen to some relaxing ambient music and write your three biggest victories of the day. Capture the things you would like to do better at and commit to do them. Scribe your commitments. Then, surrender the day and all the things you wish you'd done better. Have empathy for yourself and others, and then let the story of the day lie in the pages of the journal rather than consuming your mind. Connect with yourself through the written word.

Engage in a Relaxing and Creative Hobby like Guitar or Drawing

Morning is about productivity; evening is about creativity. Use the evening to expand your talents. Pick up a guitar (or another musical instrument), learn to draw, or do anything that's creative. You'll soon notice how therapeutic this habit becomes and how your talents will grow as a result. Don't set any expectations besides enjoyment, creativity, and learning.

Pray/Meditate

Finish the day the way you started by getting centered. Spend time closing out the day in gratitude.

Leave Your Phone Outside Your Bedroom and Sleep Peacefully

Make your bedroom a sleep sanctuary where you can get away from the mental distress of all the dings, alerts, and beeps of a cell phone. Some research suggests just having a phone in the bedroom puts the brain in a heightened state of alertness. Leave the phone in the kitchen. *If* there is an emergency, you will find out about it in the morning.

When Life Happens...

No matter how rigorous or thoughtful your self-care plan is, life will inevitably throw unexpected challenges your way. Whether in the form of sickness, lifestyle changes, emergencies, or managing relationships (just to name a few), your self-care habits can be unwound, undone, and left unattended. Everyone falls short sometimes, and that's okay. Start by having compassion for yourself when "life happens." View such interruptions not as another thing to feel bad about, but as an opportunity to learn and grow. You can emerge from the other side with even greater productivity skills, a sharper focus, and a more positive outlook. In short, when life happens, it can lead to a better life! As I wrote previously, this chapter lists an *ideal* and is full of things I try to do to take care of myself. My situation is different from yours, and it may take some time and experimentation for you to find what works for you. If a part of your initial plan ends up being unrealistic or unproductive, change it up and keep trying. Refining your routine is a part of the process. The key is to make a plan that works for you and one you'll be able to stick with.

Overcoming Pitfall 9: Protect the Asset (You)

- Create a Power Hour for yourself. You can go to the website to create your own Power Hour using the schedule builder tool. EntrepreneursParadox.com/PowerHour.

- Create a Peace Plan. The website will guide you through a peace plan and provide resources for you. EntrepreneursParadox.com/PeacePlan.

- Buy a notebook for walking meetings and journaling.

- Visit the website for additional articles and resources on Protecting the Asset. EntrepreneursParadox.com/ProtectTheAsset.

- Visit the website for the most concise and effective To-Do (and To-Don't) list available at EntrepreneursParadox.com/ToDo

Pitfall 10

No Business Acumen

One of the key indicators of success in any startup is the business acumen of the founder.

Like Thomas Watson said, having your heart in your business leads to success. Mark Patey (who you'll learn much more about in Pitfall 14) once shared, "It doesn't matter what business I run because now I know the rules of the game." These rules he speaks of constitute business acumen. Business acumen is one of the leading indicators of an entrepreneur's success. Business acumen is another way of saying business savvy or business sense. This can be expressed as having an "executive mentality" as well, which means the entrepreneur is keenly aware of how the multiple entities within a business work together and the effects each has on the business. Kevin Cope wrote the seminal book on business acumen called *Seeing the Big Picture, Business Acumen to Build Credibility, Career, and Company.* He identifies five key abilities in those with high business acumen, namely:

- See the "big picture" of the organization—how the key drivers of the business relate to each other, work together to produce profitable growth, and relate to the job.

- Understand important company communications and data, including financial statements.

- Use knowledge to make good decisions.

- Understand how actions and decisions impact key company measures and leadership objectives.

- Effectively communicate ideas to other employees, managers, executives, and the public.

I highly recommend purchasing Kevin's book. For our purposes, let's take a look at a couple of key company measures: KPIs (key performance indicators or key drivers) and being able to read and understand financial statements.

In Pitfall 6: Wearing All the Hats, I advised that an accountant or bookkeeper is the first, most important hire. Once you have an accountant in place, set aside four hours with them and ask them to teach you how to read your financial statements. If you still have questions, schedule another session. Keep going until you are intimately familiar with your numbers by asking them:

- To explain what each line means and what data is behind the line item.

- What happens to the company if each number goes up or down.

- How the numbers relate to each other.

- How to differentiate and start spotting trends.

- What lines are danger signs for the health of the company.

Remember that this book is not an accounting book and we're not going to go in-depth into each line item of a balance sheet or the profit and loss statement. Understanding this information is critical to your long-term success, however. I'm sure you'd rather be coming up with the next big idea or out in the workshop creating, tinkering, and innovating than looking at numbers. But if you don't understand the numbers, you can't understand the health of your company.

In my case, I loved playing with the marketing and creating new products. I severely neglected the part of the company that mattered for growth, however. I'll never forget the first time I met with an investment group. I was panicked because I didn't have any idea about the questions they were asking. Questions like: what's your EBITDA, CAC, and CLTV? They were asking what my profit margins were and I had no idea.

I reached out to an accountant I used to play online chess with, and I asked, "What is net vs. gross? What is this term they keep saying over and over again, EBITDA, and why is it so important?" Not knowing the answers put me in a really weak position with investors. I didn't realize at the time that I needed to be both informed and conversant with key metrics as well as being innovative and creative. I had been wrongly worried that if I focused on the numbers, I wouldn't be able to come up with the "cool" stuff too. The truth is, the cool stuff, the innovative things, and the creative side will always be there for us despite having to stretch our skills and learn to be conversant around the business drivers that matter.

Let's be honest: the numbers are easy to neglect because you've most likely never dealt with that side of things. Like me, you probably didn't go to school for accounting or finance, and it might all be a little intimidating at first. But by putting in the work to understand the financial statements and KPIs of your business, you'll free up your mind for more creativity. Once you remove the worry, concern, and ambiguity behind them, there's more room for creativity, innovation, and ingenuity. And if you don't learn how to read a balance sheet and profit and loss (P&L) statement, you'll be far less likely to know which levers to pull to make your business more profitable or which hard decisions to make when the time comes—and it always does.

Key Performance Indicators

Key performance indicators (KPIs) are like a temperature gauge for your company's health. On the way to the top of Kilimanjaro, we continually measured our blood oxygen levels. Understanding how saturated (or unsaturated) our blood was throughout the trip was critical to whether or not we reached the summit. The higher the mountain, the more important it is to understand vital statistics. Not only is it critical to achieving the goal, but it's also a happiness indicator. The lower the oxygen in the blood, the more miserable the trip and the more likely hypoxia was setting in. There were a few other health-related indicators that showed how we were doing as we progressed up the mountain, and we constantly asked each other these questions:

- Do you feel nauseated?

- Do you have a headache?

- Do you feel confused or disoriented?

- Are you coughing or wheezing?

- Any bluish skin, fingernails, or lips?

- What's your heart rate?

We continually checked our health as we climbed. We checked heart rate, breathing, skin tone, pupil dilation, hydration, cognition, and nausea. The most important factor by far was blood oxygen levels—it is literally a predictor of life or death.

This is the same as in business. Some factors show the health of your business every step of the way, others are longer-term and can even predict future success. Both types of indicators are vital to making it to the summit and avoiding the risk of dying somewhere along the trail. Each group in the company (marketing, sales, product dev, etc....) will most likely have their own measurements, but they'll all roll up into the core set of KPIs for the company. I am constantly amazed at how many travelers on the entrepreneur's journey don't check their vital signs as they climb. I used to be one of them.

Without a clear understanding, you'll often feel like you can't breathe as you enter what I'll call entrepreneurial hypoxia—the company is slowly dying, and you are never really sure why. Creating trackable KPIs will alleviate your symptoms and give you a clear direction of how to make course corrections. Sometimes you need to take a minute and acclimate to the elevation. Sometimes you have more energy than usual and can quicken the pace. The only way to know this is by tracking.

There are six main reasons to track KPIs:

1. To monitor company health.

2. To measure progress toward the goal.

3. To analyze patterns over time and create an environment of recognition.

4. To make adjustments as needed to stay on target.

5. To identify problems and find opportunities.

6. To strengthen employee morale by making KPIs visible.

Knowing the Right KPIs to Track

"Cash flow: The amount of cash (realized revenue) coming into and out of (expenses) a business."

"Runway: The length of time a company will remain financially solvent, without raising more money at the current spend rate."

"Burn Rate: The rate at which a startup spends its financing. It is often considered a measurement of negative cash flow."

As you make your way up the entrepreneurial mountain, only track the absolute essentials; otherwise you and the rest of the company will get data overload. Too much data becomes useless. It can't be consumed effectively. Tightly track the most important KPIs and let the rest go. A great list of KPIs can be easily obtained by talking to any investment group, and they'll likely all give the same list because these metrics are the ones that are the heart of any successful business. I am going to break them into three groups: surviving, thriving, and arriving (equity event). Depending on where you are and where you want to be, that will determine how in depth you need to dive into this chapter.

Here are some of the most important KPIs to track for the company as a whole:

- **Survive**
    - Cash Flow
    - Sales Cycle
- **Thrive**
    - Year-Over-Year (YoY) Trends
    - Growth Rate
    - Revenue, Profitability, Profit Margin, and EBITDA
    - Conversion Rate
    - Pricing

- **Arrive**

  - Customer Acquisition Costs (CAC)

  - Lifetime Value (CLTV)

  - CAC/CLTV Ratio

  - Churn Rate (Customer Retention/Attrition)

  - Customer Satisfaction

Cash Flow

When I started my first company, I swung between being Daddy Warbucks one month and destitute the next. One month, I would have more money than I'd ever had in my life, and the next I would be praying we could make payroll. I didn't have an understanding of cash flow. You may have heard the saying, "Cash Flow is King!" for a very good reason. 82 percent of businesses fail because of cash flow problems.[24] Understanding cash flow is critical to the long-term and short-term health of the company. Many entrepreneurs overestimate how much money is coming in and underestimate the amount of expenses going out. This creates a deficit that can hurt, cripple, or even kill the company.

The definition of cash flow is: "The total amount of money being transferred into and out of a business, especially as affecting liquidity." An easier way to say this is: Cash flow is how much money is coming in to cover the bills going out. This number can be projected based on sales activities, close ratios, employee workload, and trends. There are five major factors that need to be understood to get a handle on cash flow: runway (cash on hand), sales cycle, project timeline, accounts receivable (AR), and accounts payable (AP).

---

24   www.nexea.co/startup-survival-rate-success-failure-statistics.

Runway means how long you would be able to pay bills if another penny never came in the door. A safe measure is to have three to six months of runway in the bank. This means if you calculate all of your monthly expenditures you can cover the bills, payroll, overhead, and a little extra for miscellaneous expenses, for at least three months. Depending on your strategy and which mountain you're climbing, you don't want to go beyond six months because then you are saving money you could be using for growth. Cash is a vehicle for growth, which can be used for innovation, sales growth, marketing tools, or office expansion. Be cautious in maintaining enough runway that the plane doesn't skid off the end, but not so much that you never take off. I've seen companies be able to adapt to a global pandemic because they had enough in the bank to make the shift. Without having this runway, other companies shut down.

If you are still in development of your product and are looking for investments to cover expenses until you launch, I suggest you take whatever your estimate to completion is and add half again as much…then multiply that by 1.5. For example, if you expect it will take a year to finish development on your product, then (12 months + 6 months) * 1.5 = 27 months. There is some danger in getting too much capital because it reduces urgency, but this can be mitigated by keeping the original date and not making public the fact that the company has enough money to extend beyond the launch date.

Why Cash Flow Is Important

Understanding cash flow is like the melatonin of KPIs. Once you understand what money is coming in and that bills will be paid on time, you will be able to sleep soundly. This metric is so important that, if you don't follow it closely, it can sink your company. This nearly happened to the most highly valued automaker, Tesla, in 2008. On Christmas Eve, the company was out of money. They hadn't

properly estimated their runway nor the cash flow. In a stroke of pure
luck and amazing timing, they received $20 million in additional
funding on Christmas Eve, followed by a $200 million loan from
the US Department of Energy. Running out of cash can happen to
anyone, but it doesn't have to happen to you.

Sales Cycle

Now that you know how long you have before running out of cash,
let's get into the meat of cash flow: understanding the sales cycle.
Sales cycle means understanding how long it takes for a sale to close
from start to finish. Is your sales cycle a single phone call or is it
eighteen months with multiple flights out to a client? With service-
based companies, this is critical to understand because often there
will be an initial payment up front for services and then payments as
the service is delivered. If it's eighteen months, you will need to have
multiple deals in the pipeline so different sales land at different times
throughout the year. If the cash coming in doesn't match the cash
going out each month, you'll be sunk. Knowing what the sales cycle is
and what the average conversion rate is will give you enough data to
estimate what money will be coming in, which you can then balance
with expenses going out. The corresponding factor is project timeline.
Without knowing both, you may not make it to the end of the project
before running out of cash.

The way to mitigate this risk is to fine-tune *project timelines* and the
bidding process. For a service company, accurate bidding is life or
death. If you underbid consistently, the company will die quickly. For
product companies, it's still critical, especially when developing new
products. The key to an accurate project timeline is tracking. The best
way to estimate a future project's length is to aggregate historical data.

How long did similar projects take in the past? Really good project management tools will make this data easily apparent.

Ask your accountant or bookkeeper to create and review a cash flow report weekly. Getting a handle on cash flow as it relates to your sales cycle will change how your business runs and how many hours of sleep you get at night. Make sure that you have a weekly report of **accounts payable** (AP), money going out, and **accounts receivable** (AR), money coming in. This is the final step once the sales cycle and project timeline are measured and predicted. The weekly AP/AR will make sure the cash flow wheels don't come off.

When dealing with investors, cash flow is a critical measurement they will inspect. If you start measuring cash flow now, you will be in a strong position in the future when discussing it with investors. They want to know that you can correctly manage income and expenses. They will be looking for someone who can make accurate financial assessments. Meeting with investors likely means you are looking for capital for growth or acquisition. In order to grow, you need to know how to measure cash flow accurately. They are going to give you a large sum of money and will want to know you will use the money judiciously. When estimating future capital needs, use the formula above to account for unknowns, challenges, unforeseen market factors, and delays.

Sales cycles are typically calculated in days for smaller-ticket items, but for larger sales they can be calculated in months as well. Use whichever metric works best for your business. For this example, we'll use days. The formula for calculating is fairly simple: add up all the days for all sales in a department, then divide that by the total number of sales.

(Total number of days for all deals) / (Total number of deals)

For example, let's assume you have five deals that take the following number of days:

- Deal 1—10 days

- Deal 2—20 days

- Deal 3—15 days

- Deal 4—10 days

- Deal 5—20 days

- Total Days—75 days

That means (75 days) / (5 deals) = 15-day average sales cycle

Why Sales Cycle Is Important

Understanding sales cycles is critical to cash flow and to the happiness of your sales team. Giving them a clear understanding of the length of time for a deal to close will set realistic expectations for the team and prevent them from getting frustrated that things are taking too long. If you see some outliers in the data, use median instead of average in your formula, otherwise you'll get skewed data. For example, if Deal 5 above took 200 days instead of 20, it would appear your sales cycle was 51 days because of a single outlier.

Year-over-Year Trends

Track cash flow weekly (using a cash flow and AP/AR report from your accountant). Track it quarterly and track it yearly. And start now. Do the same with revenue. If you don't have a revenue tracking chart like the one below, get it started now. The more data you have, the better a handle you'll have on the big picture. If you haven't been doing this, it's okay. Go back through your financial statements and start entering the data into a spreadsheet or dashboard, even if they are estimates. It doesn't have to be anything fancy or expensive to start. Google Sheets will do just fine, and I've provided a smart worksheet on the website for you to be able to punch in your numbers and generate a trend graph like the one you see here.

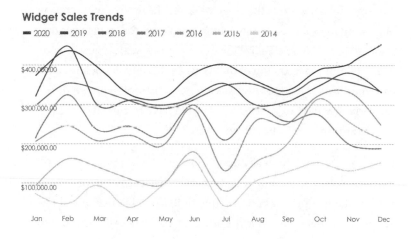

There are two big benefits to graphing your revenue like this: you can see your growth at a glance, and you can start identifying trends. For example, take a look at the month of July on the bottom four lines for the first four years, 2014–2017. There was a severe dip in revenue in the month of July *every year.* Because this trend was identified, in 2018 the company prepared and created a sales plan and pushed hard on a July-specific marketing campaign to combat the slump. Further, in the first four years, the second and third quarters (see chart below) were typically the leanest revenue of the year and put extra stress on the finances during the month of July. A big dip like this hurt the company every year. Until they started tracking the revenue trends, they weren't able to understand why and didn't know what to do about it. Once they spotted this trend, they had the power to change their circumstances. In 2018, they formulated a plan to bump up revenue in July to be able to counteract the slump. They "pumped up the slump," so to speak. Instead of falling victim to the month of July, they started marketing a huge promotion to take place at the end of June and into July, and it worked. They sent out email blasts, pushed hard on social media, had a killer deal running in July, added extra incentives for the sales team, and even added a trade show during this time. By being proactive, they were able to reverse the trend. This company sold yearly subscriptions, so each following year the company was able to stabilize the month of July with renewals and then add more sales on top of that. This could only happen because they knew their sales cycle—that sales typically took between thirty and forty-five days to close, so they would have to run all of their promotions in June to be able to close in July.

The ideal scenario is a steady uphill slope with a few peaks along the way. The reality is revenue is cyclical. Which is okay. Anytime you see a valley like July in the chart, it's time to sharpen the pencil and make a plan. Remember, you have the power to stabilize cash flow. But to do so, you have to have the knowledge and insight that comes with measuring this critical KPI.

QUARTERLY CASHFLOW TRENDS

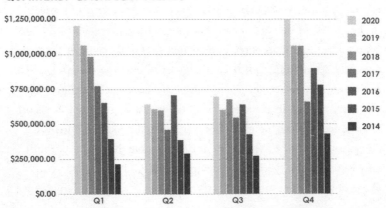

This chart shows the quarterly revenue trends. It's easy to see that Q1 and Q4 are the healthier quarters, and Q2 and Q3 are the leaner quarters. Another way to stabilize cash flow is to pay bills when the money is available and conserve cash during the lower sales months. In this case, optional expenses like company parties, bonuses, and added incentives can be distributed in the winter months when the cash is more readily available. This company ended up paying the majority of yearly expenses like software licenses, trade show registrations, SAAS renewals, and other bills when they had the money, rather than being hit with large bills in July when the revenue wasn't coming in. Most companies will work with you to arrange the timing of payments so you can distribute the expenses more evenly with the incoming revenue.

Why Trends Are Important

Trends are a big beautiful spotlight on your year-over-year financial position. When you see the cyclical trends, you will be able to address them from an informed and preparatory stance. You will be able to stabilize cash flow and know where you can increase monthly efforts.

Growth Rate

We talk about growth rate in Pitfall 3: Pulling a Goal Out of Thin Air. The formula for Year-over-Year (YoY) Growth Rate again is:

$$((\text{This Year} - \text{Last Year}) / \text{Last Year}) * 100$$

Tracking growth rate isn't difficult, and you can do so monthly or quarterly. Remember that growth rate is always presented as a percentage. For example, September had a 40 percent YoY growth. If you're applying to be on the Inc. 5000 list, you'll be asked for your three-year growth rate, which is calculated the same way with the "Last Year" being substituted by "Three Years Ago." Venture capital and private equity will look for at least a 20 percent growth rate. Another name for this is compound annual growth or CAGR.

As an early stage start-up, you are expected to grow at really exceptional rates, well beyond the 20 percent. Investment groups will often expect 60-90 percent CAGR. One investment group reported that, in order to get an investment with their firm, you would need the following YoY CAGR in the following industries.

High Tech: 70–90 percent

Manufacturing: 30–50 percent on $20 million rev

Consumer Goods: 50–80 percent

Medical: 30–50 percent

Financial Tech: 60–90 percent YoY CAGR

Excluding seed funds and pre-revenue investment, your average Venture Capital or Private Equity Fund will look for at least a 20 percent growth rate. This number changes so much from fund to fund that you will want to do your homework before seeking investment. While 20 percent CAGR is the minimum, in many cases a slam dunk would be 60–90 percent.

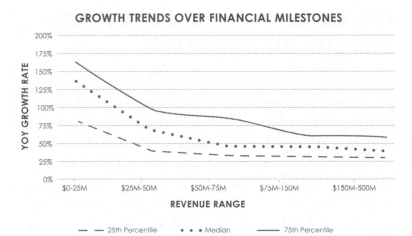

GROWTH TRENDS OVER FINANCIAL MILESTONES

Why Growth Rate Is Important

Growth rate is important to you and anyone interested in investing in the company. The faster your company is growing the more attention it will garner, which leads to additional investment from interested parties, which in turn allows the company to grow even faster. Growth rate is a general indicator of company and market segment health. The percentages will naturally and gradually slow as you continue to grow because it is a lot easier to go from $200,000 to $600,000 than it is to go from $2 million to $6 million. The stronger your growth rate, the better positioned you will be to negotiate when you do get investment. You will give away less of the company because high-growth-rate companies are desirable for venture capital and private equity.

Revenue, Profitability, Profit Margin, and EBITDA

These four terms are important to understand in relation to each other. Gross revenue, net profit, and profit margin will help you guide your company on a daily basis and can be found on an income statement. EBITDA is used when talking to investment groups and is a way venture capital and private equity groups like to compare two companies' financial health across geographies, tax jurisdictions, or capital structures. If at any point you deal with investors, you will need to know EBITDA. Ask your accountant to include this number in your financial statements so you can become familiar with it over time (it isn't typically included but can fit nicely).

Gross revenue is the total amount of income to the business. Net profit is:

(total amount of income)—(the total number of expenses)

Net profit shows how profitable the company is. You will often hear the term "top-line" and "bottom-line" revenue, and these come from the income statement and are literally the first (top) line or gross sales and the last (bottom) line or net income (also called net profits or net earnings). When companies talk about top-line growth, they mean an increase in the total revenue due to increased sales. When they talk about bottom-line growth, they're referring to growth in profitability, increased operating efficiencies, and better cost management. Here is an example:

INCOME STATEMENT *(numbers in thousands)*

Revenue	**$5,000**
Cost of Goods Sold (COGS)	$2,000
Gross Income	**$3,000**
Expenses	
Marketing & Promotions	$300
General & Administrative	$400
Depreciation	$100
Interest	$200
Total Expenses	**$1,000**
Earnings Before Tax	**$2,000**
Taxes	$500
Net Income	**$1,500**

The chart above shows top-line revenue of $5,000 and a bottom-line profit of $1,500.

Profit margin can be expressed in several ways.

- Net profit margin: The overall profit margin for the company as a whole.

- Gross profit margin: The profit margin for a single product or service.

- Operating margin: Another name for EBIT represented as a percentage. Notice the DA is missing, which means it doesn't include depreciation or amortization.

- EBITDA: How much your company earns before accounting for nonoperating expenses, represented as a dollar value.

Income Statement	
Revenue	$150,000
Cost of Goods Sold (COGS)	$55,000
Gross Profit	**$95,000**
Expenses	
Salaries and Benefits	$25,000
Rent and Overhead	$10,000
Depreciation & Amortization	$15,000
Operating Expenses	**$50,000**
Operating Profit	**$45,000**
Operating Profit Margin	**30.00%**
Interest	$4,000
Other	$6,000
Total Expenses	**$60,000**
Earnings Before Tax	**$30,000**
Taxes	$10,000
Net Earnings	**$20,000**

Here are the formulas for each of these different forms of margin.

Net Profit Margin:

(Net Income / Net Sales)*100

Broken out, it looks like this:

((Total Revenue-Business Expenses) / (Total Sales—Discounts/ Returns & Allowances)) *100

Here's an example: If your business had a net income of $100,000 and your net sales were $300,000, you would have a net profit margin of 33 percent.

($100,000 / $300,000) * 100 = 33 percent

Gross Profit Margin:

((Retail Price—Materials and Labor) / Retail Price)*100

For example, if you have a product that sells for $50, and it cost $40 to make, the gross profit margin is 20 percent because:

(($50-$40) / $50)*100 = 20 percent Gross Profit Margin

Operating Profit Margin:

(Operating Income / Revenue) * 100

Broken out, it looks like:

((Sales—Cost of Goods Sold (COGS)—Operating Expenses— Depreciation & Amortization) / Revenue) *100

For example, if you have revenue of $150,000, COGS of $55,000, operating expenses of $50,000 and depreciation & amortization of 15,000, your operating income will be $150,000—$55,000—$50,000— 15,000 = $30,000. Let's plug these numbers into the original formula:

$$(\$30,000 / \$150,000) *100 = 20 \text{ percent}$$

Every number you need for the various profit margins will be found on your profit and loss statement.

EBITDA levels the playing field when comparing two companies. EBITDA stands for "earnings before interest, taxes, depreciation, and amortization." Let's break this down. Earnings are classified as net profit. Net profit is:

(total income—total expenses)

Getting EBITDA is simple from here. All you have to do is add back in (I) interest, (T) taxes, (D) depreciation and (A) amortization:

Earnings (Total Income—Total Expenses) + Interest + Taxes + Depreciation + Amortization.

EBITDA

EARNINGS BEFORE INTEREST, TAXES, DEPRECIATION & AMORTIZATION

· ·

EBITDA = Net Income   **E = Earnings**

+ Taxes   **B = Before**

+ Interest Expense   **I = Interest**

+Depreciation & Amortization **T = Tax**

                                 D = Depreciation

                                 A = Amortization

Why is this important? Revenue, profitability, and profit margin are the main lag indicators of your company's health. You could compare these numbers to blood oxygen levels on the hike up the big mountain. If you have a 10.4 percent operating profit margin, you are doing better than most of the S&P 500 and are most likely putting money in the bank or taking distributions. Monitor these metrics closely.

Why EBITDA Is Important

EBITDA is important when negotiating with investment groups to give them a quick look at profitability on a level playing field when compared to other companies. It is used by analysts to get a quick estimate of the company's value. With this number, they will assign a valuation range based on the current multiple in your industry. EBITDA multiples are much higher than revenue multiples. For this reason, if you want to get investment or have a buyout, you want this number to be as high as possible. You can negotiate a multiple of revenue, but EBITDA is much more standard with investment groups.

Conversion Rate (Close Ratio)

Conversion rate is the number of clients who purchase versus the number who interact with your organization. The sales team will have a conversion rate separate from the website or other marketing activities like email. Measure each of these conversion rates within the department it belongs to and report back to the executive team monthly.

The formula is really simple:

(People who purchased / Total number of people contacted) * 100

For example, if your sales team contacts 1,000 people per month and 20 of those people make a purchase, your conversion rate is 2 percent:

$$(20 / 1,000)*100 = 2 \text{ percent}$$

Why Conversion Rate Is Important

In marketing, you want to have the highest conversion rate possible. In sales, this isn't necessarily always the case. Email open rates, Facebook ads, and purchases from blog posts all need the highest conversion rate possible. In sales (especially in service-based companies), conversion rate can be a market fit indicator. One service-based company I worked with had never calculated their sales conversion. When they put the numbers together, they found that they had a 70–80 percent conversion rate. They were so proud of this number. Instantly, however, I knew something was wrong. I asked to see their pricing sheet and it only took a second to see they were underbidding every job. They were the low-price leader of all the companies in the market, and so they needed to right-price themselves in the market. Knowing their conversion rate showed this fact clearly and, after doing some research, they found that they were undercutting themselves on projects. The company raised prices for their services and the win percentage (conversion rate) stabilized at about 45–50 percent.

The RAIN Group for Sales Research[25] conducted a study where they found the average win rate of sales teams to be 47 percent over 472 companies surveyed.[26] A high conversion rate on a sales team doesn't always mean an imbalance in pricing. The Elite Performers (top 7 percent) had a win rate of 73 percent and the top performers (top 20

---

25   Group, R. (n.d.). Center for Sales Research: RAIN Group. Retrieved September 12, 2020, from www.rainsalestraining.com/sales-research.

26   Schultz, M. (2016, February 16). Average Sales Win Rates: How Do You Compare? Retrieved September 12, 2020, from www.rainsalestraining.com/blog/average-sales-win-rates-how-do-you-compare.

percent) had a win rate of 62 percent. The other 73 percent only had a win rate of 40 percent so that the aggregate was 47 percent. If your sales team matches these rates, you're most likely right-priced in the market. If you are landing every bid or losing every bid, it's probably time to reevaluate pricing.

Pricing

Pricing is a key consideration for growth. Sometimes the price is too high and sometimes the price is too low. The trick is finding the sweet spot based on current market factors. The place you want to get to is the highest number of purchases at the maximum price. The economic laws of supply and demand say decreasing the price increases the number of purchases. This may be true once the price is dialed in, but please don't start with this assumption. When I first joined eLearning Brothers, we were selling a complete library with thousands of eLearning assets for $99. The price was well below market value. We increased the price to $199 and the number of new purchases went up. We added new assets and increased the price again to $299, and even more customers started signing up. We were increasing the price and increasing the number of customers in our database. We market-tested the price and found the market could bear an even higher price tag. We raised the price to $499 and even more customers began subscribing. Again, we added new assets and created a tiered pricing plan, including some lower priced options and an option for $999, and again the customer count increased. The desired result is to sell the largest number of subscriptions at the maximum price. What we found was that increasing the price didn't decrease the number of subscriptions and customers; instead it increased. Now I'm not saying the best solution will always be increasing prices. Apple has adjusted its phone prices over the years. Let's look at the iPhone and how the pricing has changed. In 2014, it started at $199–$299 and steadily increased until 2017, but then in 2018 the price came back down:

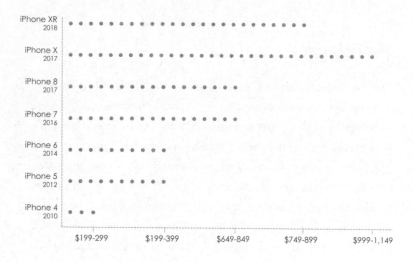

iPHONE PRICE DEVELOPMENT
Initial U.S. sales price of iPhone models (in U.S. dollars)*

*Up to and including iPhone 6 Plus, prices were only available including a cellphone contract
Sources: Apple, Statista research

Pricing is never static. Put in your calendar a yearly appointment with your team to evaluate the best pricing based on current market factors. If market factors change dramatically between now and the scheduled appointment, sit down with the team and do some market testing.

Customer Acquisition Costs (CAC)

Customer acquisition costs are calculated by adding the total sales and marketing spend to obtain a customer divided by the number of customers who purchased your product or service. For example, say you spent $100,000 on a particular online campaign and you obtained 10,000 customers. Your CAC would be $10. This number by itself doesn't really mean anything to the company without the next KPI, lifetime value. If you spend $10 to acquire a customer but they only make one purchase at $5, you're in trouble. If, on the other hand, they subscribe to a yearly service at $200 a year for an average of five years, then you have made $1,000 from a $10 CAC.

Why Customer Acquisition Costs Are Important

CAC will tell you if your business model is sustainable or if you need to change the cost of selling and marketing your goods. By breaking this down by activity, you can find out which activities have the highest ROI and focus on the ones that bring in the largest dollars for the least expense.

Customer Lifetime Value (CLTV or LTV)

CLTV will show the total expenditure per customer over their lifetime. It considers the value of a customer over the predicted customer's lifespan. This can accurately predict the revenue of a single customer over the course of the business relationship.

This formula is a multi-stage process, so let's break it down:

Step 1—Find the **Average Purchase Value** by dividing the total spend by the number of orders.

Step 2—Calculate the **Average Purchase Frequency Rate** by dividing the number of purchases per week by the number of customers.

Step 3—Take the two numbers and calculate **Customer Value** by dividing the Average Purchase Value by the Average Purchase Frequency Rate.

Step 4—Determine the **Average Customer Lifespan** by dividing the Sum of Customer Lifespans by the number of customers. For this example, the average lifespan is twenty years.

Step 5—Determine the **Customer Lifetime Value** by multiplying the Customer Value (step three) by the Average Customer Lifespan (step four).

Starbucks used this formula and found the following data about their customers:[27]

APV—$5.90
APFR = 4.2 visits/week
Customer Value = $24.30
ACL = 20 Years
CLTV = $14,099 (averaged over 3 formula types)

27   Customer Acquisition Cost: The One Metric That Can Determine Your Company's Fate. (2020, January 24).
      Retrieved September 12, 2020, from neilpatel.com/blog/customer-acquisition-cost.

AVERAGE PURCHASE VALUE	AVERAGE PURCHASE FREQUENCY RATE
$$APV = \frac{\text{Total Revenue}}{\text{Number of Orders}}$$	$$APFR = \frac{\text{Number of Purchases}}{\text{Number of Customers}}$$

CUSTOMER VALUE	AVERAGE CUSTOMER LIFESPAN
$$CV = \frac{\text{Average Purchase Value}}{\text{Average Purchase Frequency Rate}}$$	$$ACL = \frac{\text{Sum of Customer Lifespans}}{\text{Number of Customers}}$$

CUSTOMER LIFETIME VALUE

$$CLTV = \frac{\text{Customer Value}}{\text{X}}$$
$$\text{Average Customer Lifespan}$$

Why Customer Lifetime Value Is Important

The sales and marketing teams get customers in the door, but the customer success team has direct influence over the total CLTV. A good customer experience can extend the duration from four years to five years or more. Customer success can also influence the customer to increase the spend with each interaction. This is a lever to pull to increase the speed of your company growth.

CLTV:CAC Ratio

Now that you have the CAC and CLTV numbers, you can tell if you are getting customers in the door in a cost-effective way with a high ROI or not by calculating the CLTV:CAC ratio:

$$\frac{\$ \text{ Customer Lifetime Value (CLTV)}}{\$ \text{ Customer Aquisition Cost (CAC)}} = \text{Ratio}$$

Why the CLTV:CAC Ratio Is Important

Ideally, you'll want to recover the CAC in less than twelve months. The overall ratio you are looking for is a 3:1 to 5:1 ratio. This is industry specific and some reports suggest that certain industries can go as high as 10:1. Check the website at EntrepreneursParadox.com/ CAC for your industry-specific CAC/CLTV ratio.

Having three times more revenue than expense acquiring the customer is a very sustainable model. If you are below this range, you're spending too much to acquire a customer. If you are more like 5:1, you're spending too little and likely missing a large segment of customers. If your customers have a high CLTV for you, then they also have a high lifetime value to each of your competitors. It's worth paying for customers as long as the ratio stays in the sweet spot. Remember, the magic number you want to dial in is 3:1 to 5:1.[28]

Churn Rate (Customer Retention/Attrition)

Tom Henriksson, Partner at Open Ocean Capital, said, "One of the top five metrics I look for in startups that are scaling is the retention of users or customers." This is one of the trickiest KPIs to measure because there are so many factors that go into retention and attrition. I don't know anyone who claims their number is 100 percent accurate, but you can get pretty close. There is a formula for churn rate as well:

((#) Total customers lost in time period / (#) Total customers at the start of time period) *100 = Customer Churn Rate (percent)

The formula above will give you a general number for churn, but calculating retention and attrition is a little more complicated. Some factors to consider when calculating retention and attrition are:

- Customer switches companies but keeps the account
- Customer renews the account after the time period is over
- Customer changes their email address
- Customer has more than one account
- Customer renews with different contact info
- Customer moves companies but account stays with original company
- Account transfers between customers in the same company

Once you have determined how you are going to calculate retention, make sure to write down the individual formula you are using so you can elucidate the methodology to investors or partners in the future. You have an opportunity to save customers before they ever make the choice to cancel. Call them three months before they expire.

Why Churn Rate Is Important

Churn rate is one of the most important health indicators for your business. If customers are sticking around, you really have something. If there is a mass exodus, you need to make some quick adaptations. A massive change in churn can indicate a few possible scenarios:

- The product is broken or outdated.

- A competitor is quickly taking market share.

- There has been an industry shift.

- A change in customer success.

- You're targeting the wrong customer who doesn't really need the product.

- Economic recession.

In five of six of these scenarios, you have direct control to change your churn rate. Churn rate is also important because it is part of the extended CAC:CLTV ratio calculation to figure out how long a customer will be with the company.

Customer Satisfaction (CSat)

Customer satisfaction is key to churn, CLTV, CAC:CLTV ratio, and overall health of the company. It is your job to make the customer

happy; and if they are not, find out why and what you can do to
change that. Set up one of the following types of surveys for your
customers or tap into what is already online:

- Net Promoter Score

- Happy versus Unhappy

- Star Rating

- Online Reviews

- Social Media Monitoring

Why CSat Is Important

If you're actively listening to your customers, they will respond
positively. Once you hear what you can do to improve, do it. Take the
feedback and actively set a development plan to plug these holes in
the product or customer experience.

Dashboards

Now that you know what to measure and how to measure it, make
that data readily accessible. KPIs yearn for full visibility; they want
to be seen. Create dashboards that are visible to the entire company
or the relevant department. Put the dashboard in the most visible
area of your office for everyone to see. But be judicious in what you
publish—some companies publish their full financials on dashboards.
You'll need to decide what is visible to the executive team and what is
made public to the rest of the company.

EXECUTIVE DASHBOARD

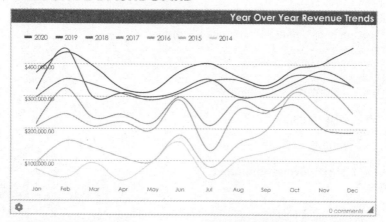

Year Over Year Revenue Trends

Legend: 2020, 2019, 2018, 2017, 2016, 2015, 2014

$400,000.00
$300,000.00
$200,000.00
$100,000.00

Jan Feb Mar Apr May Jun Jul Aug Sep Oct Nov Dec

0 comments

Revenue

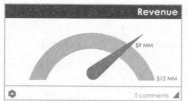

$9 MM
$12 MM

0 comments

Goal

My company will reach **$31 million** in revenue by **April 2031** when I will have an **equity event** at a **3.34x valuation** which will provide **complete financial freedom for myself and family for generations to come.** It will also provide the means to **start a nonprofit foundation** to help immigrants start businesses and earn their citizenship.

0 comments

Service Level

8/10

0 comments

Customer Retention

NEW
3,023
85.8%

RETURNING
501
14.2%

Total: 3,524

0 comments

Marketing Funnel

Interest: 120,000
Engagement: 80,000
Consideration: 32,000
Inquiry: 12,000
Proposal: 4,200
Purchase: 1,600

$380,000

0 comments

Sales Funnel

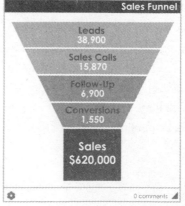

Leads
38,900

Sales Calls
15,870

Follow-Up
6,900

Conversions
1,550

Sales
$620,000

0 comments

Once the main corporate KPIs are in place, then each team will create their own KPIs. Make sure the team that can directly affect the dashboard can see it without getting up from their desks. Dashboarding is critical because it provides visibility to performance, shows the percentage of the goal met, indicates the remainder of what needs to happen, applies positive peer pressure, and allows pattern recognition. Everyone needs to see their KPI dashboard daily.

You can sign up for expensive solutions like DOMO to create a high-level dashboard with API connections and programming, or you can start with something as simple as Google Sheets and refresh the data regularly. A couple of my favorite tools are Lucid Charts and GeckoBoard.

Lead and Lag Measure

So what do you put on these dashboards? The key to tracking for the highest and fastest growth is to track lead measures rather than lag measures. Lead measures are things that affect an outcome *before* the outcome happens. Lag measures are the measures that "lag" *after* the outcome has already taken place. If you want to move the needle, use lead measures in your tracking. The king of this concept is Chris McChesney, who created the execution practice for FranklinCovey. Please read *The 4 Disciplines of Execution* by Chris, Sean Covey, and Jim Huling. Fully understanding lead and lag measures is critical for tracking any metric, and Chris is often heard saying, "Tracking with a lag measure is like trying to drive using nothing but the rearview mirror."

Here's an illustration that will help you really solidify the concept so you can put it to good use. Suppose I ask, "How do you know you are losing weight?"

The common answer is: "I stand on the scale and it tells me if I'm losing weight." This would be entirely incorrect. Look carefully at the question, "How do you know you are **losing** weight?" The question you answered was, "How do you know if you **have lost** weight?" Standing on the scale is an indicator of what has happened in the past. The question I posed was, "How do you know, in the present moment, if you are losing weight?" There is one completely accurate way to know if your body is **in the process** of shedding pounds. That is to know if the calories you are putting in your mouth are less than the calories you are burning. If you put fewer calories in your body than your body burns, then you are *losing* weight. There's no need to buy into every late-night infomercial for the miracle formula because it's simple math. In my own case, tracking my calories led to me losing over forty pounds. I've helped several friends lose up to ninety pounds using simple math and a mobile app like MyFitnessPal. The key to this step is measuring the **action** and what goes in the top of the funnel so that you can accurately predict what will come out. Most people look retroactively at what has happened in the past to try to predict the future. Predicting the future is not as difficult as most think it is. Focusing on lead measures instead of lag measures reliably predicts the outcome.

Here is a chart to illustrate the point even further with a mix of personal and business-related items.

Desired Result	Lag Measure	Lead Measure
Lose weight	What the scale says	1. How many calories you put in your mouth 2. How many calories you burn during the day
Increase sales	Total revenue brought in per month	The number of "Scheduled Next Events" each Salesperson has
Keep the car running and on the road	How often does it break down?	How often is it taken in for regular maintenance and oil change?
Increased number of users on social media	Did followers, likes, and shares go up?	Number of daily engagements with potential users
Increase customer satisfaction	NPS score	Speed of response to customer communication, number of contacts per year
Increase brand presence	Annual report of industry brand presence	Number of press releases, amount of branded material distributed at trade shows, number of ads run across social media
Health and safety	Total lost workdays, injuries/illness rate, asset/property damage	Safety/health meetings, trainings, number of inspections, risk/hazard assessment
Triathlon times	Times listed after the event for each discipline, Swim, Bike, and Run.	Number of laps in the pool, miles on the bike and training runs on the pavement

Notice that lag measures are most often discussed in past tense. Lead measures, on the other hand, are always spoken of in the present. Once more, I share the words of my friend Richard Vass: "Perplexing on the past produces pain. Fretting on the future fuels fear. Only the present provides peace and power." A good indicator that your measurement will help grow the company is if it is in the present tense. If your measurement is held in the present, then you know it will help the company grow. If it is in the past, the future is always a surprise.

Some KPIs we discussed are lag measures, but each one has corresponding lead measures. Track and display both of these metrics. For example, put on your dashboard total sales revenue as well as total "Scheduled Next Appointments."

Overcoming Pitfall 10: Develop Business Acumen

- Read this chapter, sit down with your accountant, and have him or her go over these concepts with you.

- Read this chapter again after meeting with your accountant and then explain each of these principles back to your accountant.

- Set up a recurring weekly meeting with your accountant and your executive team to review these numbers and look at which KPIs you can modify to help you reach your goal.

- Create a dashboard for the executive team and one for the company in whole.

- Schedule a yearly pricing review with your executive team.

- We have provided a spreadsheet with all the formulas prepopulated on the website. EntrepreneursParadox.com/Formulas.

- If you don't have an accountant who is readily accessible, go to the website and request a free Business Acumen consultation. EntrpreneursParadox.com/Acumen.

- Check the website for your industry-specific CAC/CLTV ratio. EntrepreneursParadox.com/CAC

- See examples of other dashboards and upload yours to help other entrepreneurs. EntrepreneursParadox.com/Dashboard

Breaking the Promise

Promises kept builds trust, affinity, and loyalty.

Most companies have a mission statement; some have a vision statement, goals and objectives with timelines, dollar values, and expected impact, but few have a promise. A promise is the basis of the customer experience, ARR (average rate of return), MRR (monthly recurring revenue), and lifetime value in a start-up business. The promise is how much the customer can trust the experience each time they interact with your business. This is accomplished through building trust with the customer by having a standardized, repeatable process. This way the customer can trust the experience will be the same without any surprises or changes.

The Promise

Having trust in the experience is different from a brand promise. A brand promise is a tagline that tries to get people to move to action. For example, Apple's brand promise is "Think Different." Geico has a great one: "15 minutes or less can save you 15 percent or more on car insurance." These are memorable taglines, but they don't talk about building a replicable business model. The promise is the user interface of your business and creating it means building a standardized methodology and process so the customers know what to expect each and every time they interact with the business. Websites have designers who are experts in UI/UX (user interface/user experience) and we can learn a lot from them. If you want to take your business to the next level, you have to fine-tune this model so that the least skilled person on your team can be put in place and the system will still work flawlessly. Most franchises spend their entire business development cycles perfecting the user experience because customers want to trust the company they're doing business with. Patrons of a fast-food restaurant want to trust that they'll get their food quickly and that it will be prepared and delivered in the same way each time. This principle is so critical that even with a decidedly unhealthy menu, a fast-food restaurant like McDonalds can become the single largest fast-food restaurant in the world. There is an unwritten promise that the customer will have the exact same experience every time they enter the franchise to buy one of their burgers. I've been to twenty-four countries, and every time I give the local golden arches my patronage (largely because I want to see how similar the experience is); whether in Morocco, Israel, Japan, Germany, Paris, Greece, or London, the experience was exactly the same. There may be local additions to the menu, like wasabi fries in Japan, but the experience is largely the same: the servers wear clean and clearly recognizable uniforms, the counters are laid out in familiar ways, the menus sit on screens above the order takers, and the fries are only allowed to sit for seven minutes before they're thrown out. Orders are placed at one counter and picked up at another, and the entire experience happens in just a few minutes. *McDonald's is successful not because they sell the best burger but because they consistently deliver on the promise.*

Another example of the impact of a promise can be found in a mortgage company which proudly displayed a wall full of thank-you cards in their lobby. After each closing, they would do several follow-up calls with customers to find out how the process was going and when they were moving into their new home. Then, on the day of the move, the mortgage company would send pizza to the house when they knew their clients would be hungry, tired, and in the midst of the moving chaos. Talk about going the extra mile! Sometimes they would even hand-deliver the pizza and welcome their former clients to their new home. This mortgage company was even known for jumping in and helping unload some of the boxes and furniture from the moving van! Word of mouth spread quickly, and the company grew. But because of the increased demand, the high-touch practice of delivering pizzas to all of their clients came to an end. I spoke with some customers and when I asked how their experience was, they said it was different the second time and they probably wouldn't use them again. And they definitely wouldn't refer them to anyone else. When I asked if they felt their mortgage rate was fair, they replied it was great. Nor were they dissatisfied with the loan origination fees or how they were treated by the employees. When I finally asked why they wouldn't use them again, they said, "There was no pizza." Unfortunately, this company's promise had been broken. Was there a guarantee that there would be pizza? No. Was there even anything written that said anything about pizza? No. There was an unspoken promise of exceptional service that went above and beyond...and when that promise didn't come to fruition, people felt let down. This is why creating a standardized system that can scale with growth is so important.

With the enormity of 36,000 locations serving over 68 million people daily, it would be impossible to keep the McDonald's promise without a standardized system. They even train owners and managers at their Hamburger U—their number-one focus is keeping that unspoken promise every time.

So how does this apply to your business? The fastest way to meet the customer promise is to plan for it:

- Be deliberate when creating your promise. Outline the complete experience from look and feel, to dialogue, to tone, to how a customer enters and leaves each interaction.

- Review the promise and make sure it is repeatable every time.

- Deliver on your promise each time.

- Ask your customers what they think the promise is.

- Adjust the system or the promise based on the feedback from customers to provide the best experience possible.

Survivorship Bias

A lot of entrepreneurs bump into a common misstep known as survivorship bias. Let me illustrate this with a story: December 7, 1941, marked a tragically historic day as Pearl Harbor was attacked, prompting the United States to enter World War II. What was not well-known was the formation of a top-secret organization called the Statistical Research Group (SRG), a block away from Columbia University in New York City.

During the war, the Allied forces were alarmed at the mortality rate of bomber crews. Even though today flying is statistically the safest form of transportation, during the war, airmen were essentially flipping a coin. Out of a thousand crew members that took to the air, 450 were killed, 60 were severely wounded, 80 entered a POW camp, and only 410 returned unscathed. Can you imagine if those were the same statistics for commercial flights today? No one would fly knowing they had a 41 percent chance of survival. And yet these brave soldiers were willing to take that risk in the fight for freedom, knowing that bombing the enemy was critical to the Allies' strategy and couldn't be stopped even though the death rate was so high.

Because they couldn't stop the bombing raids, the Navy decided they would try to figure out ways to bring more of their boys home. One idea was to armor the most vulnerable areas of the planes, but as it gained momentum, it became apparent there was a critical flaw: fully armored planes can't fly; they are too heavy, only partially armored planes can. The thought then turned to only putting armor where the planes were getting hit the most. Working with British intelligence and diagnostics, they started identifying the patterns of bullet holes on planes returning from their bombing engagements over Europe. They quickly began recognizing patterns.

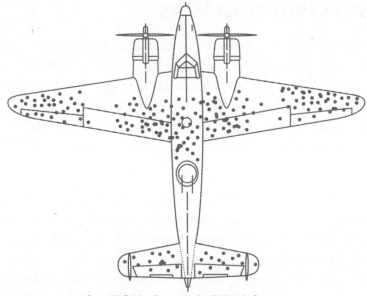

Source: McGeddon, "Survivorship Bias," Wikimedia Commons, commons.wikimedia.org/wiki/File:Survivorship-bias.png, accessed March 2019.

It was easy to pinpoint three major areas where the planes were receiving the most fire: the wings, the fuselage (body), and the elevators (tail). The Navy immediately started making plans to reinforce the planes in the susceptible areas to increase survivorship.

But just how much armor was required? They took the data to the Statistical Research Group based in Manhattan.

Luckily, a Jewish-Hungarian statistician named Abraham Wald, who had escaped Nazi-occupied Austria and made his way to America to assist in the war effort, saw the reports and the diagrams and asked a game-changing question: "Where are the missing holes?" Scratching their heads, the officers looked at each other in confusion. This was all the data they had. Wald then asked and answered the question himself: "Where are the missing holes? The missing holes are in the missing planes."

This brilliant statistician realized what no one else was seeing. The planes that landed back on the airfields and aircraft carriers were the planes that *survived*, specifically because they didn't have holes in the engines or the cockpits. The planes that were at the bottom of the ocean or ended up as rubble in a farmer's field were those with the holes in the *opposite* patterns from the surviving planes. Wald spelled out that the armor didn't need to go where the bullet holes were; it needed to go where the holes weren't. Namely around the engine powering the planes and the pilots flying the planes.

The military had uncovered the exact opposite of what they were looking for. The Navy was hoping to find the most vulnerable areas of a plane and instead found the most resilient areas that could suffer the most damage without catastrophic failure. Because of Abraham's

willingness to look at the whole picture, many lives were saved, and
he helped turn the tide of the war.

So what patterns are you looking at when it comes to your business?
You need to get the full picture before fortifying the planes.
Specifically, you need to talk to your customers and make sure
you are fulfilling the customer promise. But don't just talk to the
customers that make it back to the airfields; talk to the ones that don't
make it back.

Talk with Former Customers

Joe Gebbia, one of the founders of Airbnb, shared a story with me and
three hundred others at the Inc.com Grow Conference. The business
was taking off and they wanted to take things to the next level. To
increase sales, they turned to Paul Graham from Ycombinator, who
recommended that they "go meet the people." And so they did, asking
current and former customers what was wrong with their product.
They even stayed in the same rental properties and had breakfast with
their customers and property owners. Joe and the other founders
assumed everyone knew how to take an inviting image to highlight
the space to be rented. Instead, many of the pictures and descriptions
of the listings were poor-quality—no one wanted to rent what looked
like a dimly lit cave.

The three founders immediately went to work and started creating a
system that would ensure that every listing was welcoming and the
descriptions were accurate and safe. Because they sought out feedback
and put a new system in place, Airbnb has grown to have the largest
number of rentable rooms in the world—even more than Marriott
and Hilton.

To find out how you are doing, you need to talk to former customers and find out where all the holes are. You might be asking, "How do I find the customers that didn't make it back?" You become a student of customer retention and attrition. Luckily, your non-returning customers aren't spiraling down over Europe in a ball of flames. They are probably sitting at their desks, having a productive day at the office…not using your product or service. If you're asking, "How do I get a hold of them?" there's a bigger problem. The most valuable item any customer will ever give you is their personal information. This is so valuable, in fact, it's one of the most important things a company can gather. If you don't already, create a strategy and process for collecting customer data. This can be done during the checkout process, through blogs, or through social media, or it can be done over the phone. Securely store this information in a CRM (customer relationship management) tool like SalesForce or HubSpot. At a former company, we used single sign-on with social media to capture user data in case the person changed jobs and email addresses. These customers were never lost because we had several ways to connect with them.

Remember, your product is not your product; your promise is your product. Give your users a consistent, familiar, and enjoyable experience each time they interact with your company. It doesn't matter if customers are communicating over chat, phone, in person, email, social media, advertisements, or any other medium. Make sure they experience your company in the same way. Changing the interaction causes the user's brain to process the situation differently. Our bodies and senses are wired to detect change because change can be a sign of danger. So the more jarring the change, the more "danger" signal happens in the brain. Giving the same experience every time brings a subconscious safety the customer comes to rely on.

Overcoming Pitfall 11: Keep Your Promise

- Write down the current "Customer Experience" in detail with your team.

- Evaluate each contact point and ask if that's the experience you really want your customers to have.

- Once a quarter, schedule a full calendar day dedicated to calling customers, gathering feedback, and reviewing the data. This is something that you as the owner and founder will want to do personally at first. Once you start to dial in the process, scale back to once a year for you personally, but keep the quarterly cycle for the company.

- Create a process for contacting former customers as soon as they drop off the radar. If you have a subscription model, contact customers thirty and sixty days before they expire. This will give you important feedback and will also be a great customer retention tool.

- Play "Undercover Boss" and see if the experience is the same as the promise.

Building Not Selling

*A careful examination of blind spots will reveal they
are shaped in the same form as our past.*

A couple of years ago, a triathlon training company called Elevate
Utah wanted to see if they could transform an "average Joe" into
a winning triathlete in his age division. Elevate Utah wanted to
prove that with the right training, nutrition, and equipment, anyone
could win. The test subject was an entrepreneur who was slightly
overweight, had never cycled competitively, and was somewhat afraid
of the water because of a traumatic near-drowning experience as a
child—**me**. Keep in mind, they were not trying to see if they could get

me to *participate* in a triathlon or even *compete* in a triathlon. Their hypothesis was that they could get me to *win* a triathlon. And to up the ante even further, they believed they could accomplish this within a single year of training. It was a daunting task for me, especially the swim. I learned quickly that I wasn't a good swimmer but was a phenomenal sinker. I can sink like nobody's business.

As the test subject, I woke up six days a week between four and four thirty in the morning to train for one and a half to two hours (double that on the weekend). Progress was slow at first, but eventually, I started making headway toward the goal. Also, I happily found that I could swim without drowning and became quite excited about overcoming this fear. Months into the training, I started signing up for triathlons. Gradually, I was beginning to advance in the rankings toward the winner's circle. After doing several sprint triathlons, I decided to race in my first Olympic distance triathlon. I chose the Spudman in Idaho, mostly because the swim portion was in the Snake River, meaning the aquatic part could be fairly fast and without much effort.

My goals for each of the individual disciplines were:

1. Emerge from the water in the middle of the pack

2. Maintain a speed of at least eighteen to twenty m.p.h. on the bike

3. Pass at least a hundred people on the run

With the rest of my start group, I entered the Snake River with anxious excitement. We swam to the middle of the river and the gun went off. Swimming downstream was fantastic—it felt like I had propellers on my ankles. I caught the river's current perfectly and launched toward the finish line. Coming out of the water right in the middle of the pack was a huge improvement from when I started my training. As usual, I dizzily climbed out of the water (because of swimmer's ear) and found my bike in the transition corrals.

I changed quickly out of my wetsuit and jumped on my bike. The bike portion went well for the first ten to twelve miles but was a little rough the last half because I hadn't prepared for the distance. I knew I was losing power when people started passing me near the end of the ride, but I thought, *It's okay; the run is my strongest event and I'll crush it.*

The transition from Bike to Run went smoothly. I put on my trusty Altra Running shoes and headed out on the course. It started with a little uphill section and I was already passing people, then leveled out as I passed even more. With my goal of passing a hundred people, I was counting each "kill" as I zipped by. Before I was even halfway through the race, the count exceeded a hundred, so I decided to increase the goal to two hundred. After all, I was crushing my goal, so why not try to double it?

Thoughts traveled through my brain as I listened to the steady rhythm of my feet on the road: *This is amazing. It really isn't even as hard as I thought it would be. I wonder why it's not harder?* I continued counting silently, 110, 120, 130, *uh-oh a large group of people, quick, count fast*, 155, 175, 190, 200, 210, etc.… Because I reached my initial goal and even surpassed the much larger secondary goal, I decided to stop counting with a mile left to go.

I turned down the grassy hill toward the big inflatable arch at the finish line, feeling like I had made up a lot of distance from the swim and bike. When the finisher medal was placed around my neck, I felt a great measure of satisfaction and confidence, both with my run and the race overall. After making my way through the finishers corral, I found the results stand.

I looked at my splits for each discipline and realized that, although I had passed over two hundred people on the run, I had actually run at a much slower pace than normal. My pace was so slow, in fact, it was less than a normal workout. No wonder it felt so easy. I HAD MEASURED THE WRONG THING! I was counting a metric that didn't, and couldn't, get me to the winner's circle: people, instead of speed. In order to win, there was really just one piece of data that I needed to focus on: my mile pace. Instead of passing hundreds of people (at a slow pace), I needed to run at a fast pace. In fact, I needed to run a low 7:00 mile or faster, regardless of how many people I passed. Spending mental effort counting my "kills" took up focus that could have been concentrated on how fast I was actually running. My feelings of victory quickly deflated when I realized I was measuring the wrong objective.

Needless to say, it took several more triathlons before I stood atop the winner's podium.

So, how does this apply to business? It's easy to get caught up in measuring the things that have little to no effect on achieving the *big* goal.

Let's take a look at some of the common mistakes as they show up in marketing, sales, and strategy.

Marketing

Let's take a look at just one marketing metric that people often get obsessed with: the number of followers on social media. Many companies chase this rabbit without ever getting closer to the finish line. Building as many social media followers as possible is a great goal as long as the followers are engaged and converting to dollars. Just like my race, counting people felt good and it gave me a false sense of accomplishment. Getting another 10,000 followers is fantastic because now you have the communications channel to reach another 10,000 people and share your message...if...*big if*...those people are engaged in a meaningful way. Having 500,000 followers that never respond to a tweet or Instagram post is the same as having zero followers. You want to connect, not just contact; *engage* and not just count. There are several people and companies that do this really well. One example is the world's youngest billionaire, Kylie Jenner. She tweets or throws an Instagram post about a limited-time release of a product in her Kylie Cosmetics line, and it sells out in less than a minute. That's the right metric to be measuring.

I had the opportunity to visit Dell's Social Media Command Center a few years back, and at the time they were accurately attributing over $50 million in sales to Twitter alone. That is the right metric. Marketing is one of the easiest areas in a company to chase red herrings, and social media is a classic example. For my entire career, I have heard people say it's impossible to measure return on investment (ROI) for trade shows. This statement is not true anymore. With my company eLearning Brothers, we figured out the formula so that when we left the trade show floor, we knew to the penny the number of direct purchases, invoices, and purchase orders we had secured. Marketing must be quantified to be effective.

Advertising is an area that people have traditionally taken a lazy marketing approach toward and not measured effectively. It's the one area that people have chalked up to brand recognition and awareness instead of hard metrics that move the company's and the entrepreneur's overall goals forward. So how do you know what to measure? How do you know if you are hitting the mark? Here are four questions that will guide you in making marketing decisions. If you ask yourself these four questions sequentially, every time you have a critical decision, your start-up will begin to grow at faster rates and you won't have to wonder if you're doing the most important marketing activities for your new business's growth.

- Does this marketing activity increase the revenue of my start-up?

- Does this marketing activity increase the profitability of my start-up?

- Does this have the highest ROI of any activity I can do?

- How do I measure the three items above?

Let's apply these questions to one of the marketing channels we discussed above: social media.

Q: Does getting Instagram followers affect revenues positively?
A: No, not directly.

Q: Does getting Instagram followers increase profitability?
A: No, not directly.

Q: Does getting Instagram followers have the highest ROI of any activity I can do?
A: I don't know; I haven't associated it with revenue.

Q: How do I measure the revenue, profitability, and ROI of getting more followers?
A: With just followers, I can't. (But asking this question will lead you to a deeper level of understanding where your marketing time and dollars are going and how effective you are as an entrepreneur and marketer).

Hopefully you can see the pattern: there is a funnel at work and measuring the top is simply not enough. This is where we go from being a lazy marketer to being an entrepreneur with true vision. Stop measuring the top of the funnel alone (followers). Once you're measuring all the way to the end of the row (revenue), profit and

ROI will flow naturally. Measuring social media followers is only the first step. I've seen entrepreneurs proudly boast with head held high that they have a large Instagram following. If that is where they stop measuring, then the entrepreneur missed the mark entirely. An effective entrepreneur/marketer will connect followers through every part of the funnel and end up with a revenue number.

Back to Dell Technologies and their Social Media Command Center. I saw how effective they were with conversions through Twitter, Facebook, etc.... It was amazing. Sure, they knew how many followers they had and how many likes they were getting for their posts, but they didn't focus on those numbers. I don't think I even heard the "follower" stat more than once the entire time I toured the facilities. Instead, they talked about how much revenue they were making from each of the channels. Instead of boasting about how a lot of people thought they were cool and wanted to follow them, they were singularly focused on how that related to dollars in the bank.

The point of getting followers on any social media platform is to advance them to the next step. Don't get me wrong, I'm not saying to stop all social media activity—the opposite is in fact true. Social media is a great channel to create exposure and engagement. What I am saying is that getting followers is just the top of the funnel (ToFu). Followers need to turn into buyers at the bottom of the funnel (BoFu). Following is nice, engagement is better, but conversion is the goal. Here is an example of a funnel for social media:

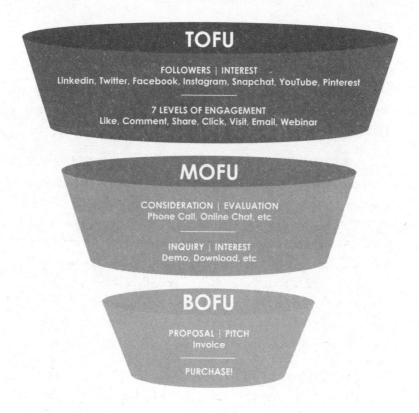

The top of the funnel (ToFu) is awareness. The middle (MoFu) is interest, engagement, and consideration. The bottom of the funnel (BoFu) is decision and conversion.

An effective entrepreneur/marketer will measure each of these segments. For example, if you know that out of 10,000 followers, 500 will engage at any given time, and out of the 500, 25 will show some sign of interest or inquiry, and out of the 25, two will make it to the purchase stage, then you can look at each of the levels in the funnel and start fine-tuning. One tweak, such as increasing the conversion rate from 500 engaged followers to 600, will then flow down the pipe and result in higher revenue overall.

Using this approach, the next time you go into a meeting to report on marketing activity, you will be able to say, "Marketing produced $500,000 in revenue" instead of "Marketing got 100,000 new followers."

After revenue comes profitability and ROI. Profitability is a simple formula of removing the cost of marketing activities from the revenue those activities produced. ROI is making profitability a percentage or a multiple instead of a dollar value. Another way of putting it is, how many dollars did you stick in the top of the marketing machine and how many additional dollars came out the bottom? So, if you spent $1 and made $5, then your ROI is 4x or 400 percent and you made $4 profit.

$$\frac{\text{(RETURN-INVESTMENT) (\$)}}{\text{INVESTMENT}} * 100\% = \text{ROI}$$

$$\frac{(\$5 \text{ REVENUE} - \$1 \text{ EXPENSES})}{\$1 \text{ EXPENSES}} * 100\% = 400\% \text{ or } 4x$$

Finally, the last step in becoming an effective entrepreneur marketer is to compare all of your activities and look at which activity has the highest ROI and invest more dollars into that activity. Another important factor is to evaluate all the funnels and see if you can create higher ROI for other activities,

Let's ask those same four questions again, but with the entire social media funnel considered:

> **Q:** Does the social media funnel affect revenues positively?
> **A:** Yes, we now have an additional $500,000 in sales directly attributed to social media.

Q: Does getting social media increase profitability?
A: Yes, we had a profit of $400,000 by spending $100,000 in expenses.

Q: Does flowing customers through the social media funnel have the highest ROI of any activity I can do?
A: Currently, it is the number-two highest-ROI-producing activity for my start-up. I'll continue these activities and do even more.

Q: How do I measure the revenue, profitability, and ROI of getting my complete social media funnel?
A: 100,000 followers in the ToFu equals 10,000 engaged followers in the MoFu and produces 500 buyers per month in the BoFu; each of these buyers spent $1,000 on your product equaling $500,000 in revenue and $400,000 in profit or a 4x (400 percent) ROI.

With these numbers, you can now confidently say that you are measuring the marketing metrics that matter in your start-up. I would love to write an entire book around marketing and how to run effective campaigns. Who knows, maybe I will. For now, here are some of the action items you can implement.

Marketing Quick Wins in Building Your Funnel

Top of the Funnel

If you are just getting your business off the ground, start with the ToFu activities. Here are the first things I suggest to get the marketing engine started:

- Build a website to promote and sell your products. Make sure you have a really good e-commerce engine that is simple and usable.

- Sign up for all the social media channels with a consistent handle (the shorter the better).

  - LinkedIn

  - Facebook

  - Instagram

  - Twitter

  - Pinterest (Yes, Pinterest)

  - YouTube (one of the most critical)

  - Snapchat

  - Etc....

- Post daily to each of the channels. You can do this easily with some simple social media distribution tools like Hootsuite, Sprout Social, or some of the larger tools like HubSpot or SalesForce. Make sure you are giving to your customers. Don't be a "Me Monster." It's great to highlight products and give offers, but the most effective way is to give content customers like and will want in their feeds regularly. Doing this will allow you room to pop an offer in their feed without being obtrusive. A good rule of thumb is ten to one post: at least ten posts that are just for your customers' enjoyment or benefit before posting one asking for them to engage.

- Start a blog and write at least once a week. This will drive customers' affinity. Release your post at the same time every week. For example, always launch your posts on Tuesday at nine o'clock.

- Webinars—free educational webinars.

Middle of the Funnel

If you already have your messaging out in the world, start honing the middle of the funnel (MoFu). Make sure you are capturing personal data when someone engages with your company. Here are some activities and content customers can start to engage with:

- Case Studies
- Fact Sheets
- White Papers
- Infographics
- Email Drip Campaigns
- Newsletter
- Webinars—Solutions Overviews

Bottom of the Funnel

This is where things begin to get good. This is where the money starts to come in. If you haven't already by this point, get a marketing automation system like HubSpot or SalesForce which will also have a customer relationship management (CRM) tool.

- Webinars—Product Demos
- Online Chat
- Sales Calls
- Trainings
- Proposals
- Pitches
- Invoices

You'll notice the BoFu has a lot of activities that are less marketing
activities and more sales related, especially if the product or service
is a high-ticket item. This leads us into our next section, focused on
another oft-forgotten item in the entrepreneur's journey—sales.

Sales

Many companies look at contacts, leads, and names in a database
as key metrics in sales. I have heard from many young companies
how excited they are about a lead they just put into Salesforce. The
excitement comes because the lead has a big name like Walmart,
Amazon, or some other large company. During my time at
FranklinCovey, I had the chance to work with an amazing sales
executive named Shawn Moon. When I asked him who the number-
one salesperson was and what that person was doing, he pointed
out Gretchen Gill. Gretchen was (and is) on a mission to "Create
the Ultimate Competitive Advantage Through the Development of
Your Organization's Greatest Asset—Your People." I flew to the East
Coast to meet her and asked what she was doing that was so special.
She shared her normal workday with me. She was only a couple of
years into her tenure at FranklinCovey, and Gretchen spent three to
four hours meeting with clients and potential clients. Then she would
spend the remainder of the day filling the pipeline through phone
calls. Keep in mind this is a multi-million-dollar salesperson who is
on the phone for hours each day.

To be candid, this was not what I expected. After analyzing the entire
sales force, Shawn helped me see that one of the most important
metrics to sales success was how many phone calls were made in a day
which resulted in future meetings. At the time, I didn't understand
the amazing level of persistence and diligence Gretchen had for phone
calls…that is, until I recently spoke with Cameron Baird, the COO of

Griffin Hill (one of the premier sales training companies in the US).
I asked Cameron what the single most important stat is to measure
in viewing the ongoing success of a salesperson or sales team. His
response was instant: "Scheduled Next Events."

There are several key components to a Scheduled Next Event:

- Date

- Time

- Location

- Purpose, Mutually Understood

Date and time are pretty straightforward. Location can either be a
physical location, phone call, or video conference. In-person meetings
are always the most effective. Video conferencing comes in second
place and phone calls are the final option. Regardless of location, the
key is to make sure the calendar invite is very specific and eliminates
any confusion. If the location is a video conference call, make sure
the other party has all the necessary links, cameras, technology, and
downloads. Instructions can be clearly spelled out directly in the
invitation. Purpose, Mutually Understood, is key in successful sales. It
alleviates friction in the sales process, sets the expectation toward the
close, and qualifies the interest of the prospect. This step takes some
clarification with the client.

The principles that make Scheduled Next Events so effective include
the Law of Human Performance. People perform to deadlines; it's
just a fact. So, create a deadline called a calendar invite. How many
times have you seen an old friend and announced, "Hey, let's get
together sometime," and then promptly forgot to put something on
the calendar? Those meetings rarely, if ever, happen. Next time you
see one of those friends, pull out your phone and apply the Date,
Time, Location, and Purpose Mutually Understood principles. Done
within a sales context, this gives the salesperson credibility, saves

time and headache, and dramatically increases the likelihood of advancing the sale.

An example of an effective Scheduled Next Event is:

> Salesperson: Let's get together to talk about your goals and priorities... How does Thursday morning look for you?

> Client: Yeah, Thursday morning is open.

> Salesperson: Great, would nine or ten o'clock work better to dig into your priorities and identify how we can help you achieve your goals?

> Client: Nine o'clock works great.

When Griffin Hill does their research within companies, they find that, even though sales teams think they are being effective, it is often less than 10 percent of the current prospects with a Scheduled Next Event that includes all four elements. Sales teams can become predictive about sales when they implement the type of sales system Griffin Hill teaches. In most cases, salespeople can speed up the sales cycle by as much as 66 percent. The key is getting standardized systems to be fully integrated into sales teams. Dr. Scott Baird, founder of Griffin Hill, said, "We are all the product of the systems we employ. We can never reach a level of achievement higher than the quality of our systems."

Finally, I asked Cameron in one sentence what is the most important thing he wanted to tell sales managers and sales teams. His thoughtful response was, "Keep forward sales momentum by continually having a minimum of fifteen Scheduled Next Events."

Strategy

Determine which of your activities will be the highest value for
the company overall, but don't get this confused with an ROI
performance metric. This can be an activity with an immediate
ROI or an activity that won't produce an ROI until much later. For
example, one of my coaching clients, Scott Severe, had a software
company that facilitated laborers, construction companies, and
contractors with billing and appointments, etc. They had grown
incrementally for years, but one of his top concerns was that their
software and apps weren't up to the same level as their competitors.
As a result, he was pouring money into development and was
incessant about keeping up with the latest trends and features of his
biggest competitor.

When we looked at Scott's goals, it became clear that revenue
growth was at the top of the list, yet he was pouring all his resources
into development. I asked one simple question: "What if you
stopped developing?"

After the initial shock wore off, this wise and humble CEO thought
about it and replied, "We could have a viable product for over a year
and a half before it became outdated."

The next question changed the thinking of the company completely.
I asked, "What if you spent the money you had earmarked for future
development on sales instead?" The last several years in this company
was literally the definition of bootstrapping. Every extra penny went
right back into development. I suggested they look at sales as the
highest-value activity and use the proceeds from the additional sales
they landed to fund additional development…if needed. The key
was getting the sales *first*, and once a profitable margin was attained,
funnel the money back to development. This turned out to be the
largest growth activity in the company's history. They went from

small, incremental year-over-year growth to doubling revenue in one year's time. The company they were always trying to keep up with ended up buying them because of their rapid growth.

When you, the entrepreneur, set your sole focus on the *big goal*, the one that can transform your start-up, and remove all the small distracting goals, you will achieve incredible things and the company will be able to experience massive growth.

Go Big or Go Home

Between my time starting my own companies, I had the opportunity to work for one of the most prolific leadership companies, FranklinCovey. The most significant insights I gained were taught to me by Scott Miller, author of *Management Mess to Leadership Success* and other successful books. We were discussing trade show strategies and were considering attending a yearly conference. We were discussing the size of the booth we'd employ, such as a well-branded ten-by-ten booth or maybe even a ten-by-twenty booth. Scott halted the conversation and boldly declared, "It's time we go big or go home. It is not enough to just show up; we need to make a splash and make a difference."

With Scott's *go big or go home* mantra ringing in our ears, we ended up with a forty-by-forty booth that hosted a twenty-foot-tall jumbotron made of synchronized Amazon Kindle Fires. We gave all 256 Kindle Fires away during the show, and in return we had almost nine thousand people register for one of our events.

At that same conference I ran into a couple friends, Andrew and Shawn Scivally. They had started a business called eLearning Brothers in their basements, focused on helping companies get training online.

A few years later, I consulted with them and ended up joining the
company as a part-owner. I carried the *go big* lesson with me, and
when it was our turn to attend a trade show, we asked ourselves:
"As a start-up, how can we afford to create a massive presence like
FranklinCovey did?" How do we pay for the cost of going big? The
answer was we couldn't buy hundreds of Amazon Kindles to give
away at multiple trade shows. Our revenue wasn't a quarter of a
billion dollars. We didn't have the cash to do what FranklinCovey
did, but we did have other things. We had people, we had a ton of
creativity, we had excitement and energy, we had our orange color
used in our recognizable brand, we had partners, and we had Bro-
Bands: orange '70s-style sweatbands.

We put pencil to paper and started figuring out the costs. The floor
space would be one of the most expensive pieces, and we would have
to take a risk on that. The booth backdrop would be fairly cheap,
and we could create some killer graphics. Transportation costs were
pretty low as the first show was in Las Vegas, which was a six-hour

drive from our headquarters near Salt Lake City. We decided to drive the entire company down in some oversized vehicles (my business partner had a twelve-seater van to transport his nine kids around in). Our goal was to flood the trade show with a sea of orange.

At the event, we gave away a thousand Bro-Bands, then we would seek out people in the halls wearing them and gave a "Two-Dolla Holla" by passing out a two-dollar bill in thanks for the attendee wearing our swag. Each time someone purchased our library subscription, we would do a slow clap and hoot and holler, which would inevitably get more people to come to our booth and sign up. Finally, we asked each of our partners to give away a subscription to their software or service and ran a giveaway. Because of our partners, we were able to give away over $20,000 in prizes.

Did you catch a very important detail in the description above? We did something no one else was doing, and most still don't. We had customers purchasing our product on the trade show floor, swiping credit cards at our booth. The first show was so successful, we realized we had to keep attending conferences because the return on investment was so high. By going big, we vaulted past most of the steps in the marketing funnel and went directly to making a purchase…and it worked! Consider the change in crowd size from the first booth picture to this one:

Going big or going home isn't always about money. If you have the resources of a FranklinCovey, you can build an entire wall of tablet devices and then give them away. Or you can flood a trade show in a sea of color that reflects your brand and doesn't cost near as much. Either way, be creative, make good use of the resources you have, and never settle for going small when you can go big instead.

Overcoming Pitfall 12: Drive Revenue

- Write down the answer to this question: "If we were to stop building or adding to our product today and used those dollars on sales and marketing, what would happen to revenue?"

- Evaluate your marketing plan and ask yourself for each activity, "What can we do to Go Big or Go Home?"

- If you have an MVP (minimum viable product) then ask yourself, "Which activities will produce the quickest path to additional revenue?" If the product is not ready to be released, continue focusing on the product.

- Create a three, six, and twelve-month marketing plan. You can find example marketing plans on EntrepreneursParadox.com/MarketingPlan.

- Evaluate your marketing plan and ask yourself for each activity, "What can we do to Go Big or Go Home?"

- Create a three-month sales ramp-up strategy. You can find example sales strategy on EntrepreneursParadox.com/SalesStrategy.

Pitfall 13

A Thousand Great Ideas

"The idea that we're going to accomplish more by doing multiple things at the same time is false."

—DAVE CRENSHAW

Thomas Edison once said, "Opportunity is missed by most people because it is dressed in overalls and looks like work." This isn't your problem. You know how to work: you have a relentless drive. You love to solve problems and come up with amazing solutions, and you're willing to put in the hours because you see the vision of what your dream can become. You and Edison might have experienced the same dilemma, though. Because you're willing to work and because you aren't scared of creating an amazing dream, you bump into opportunity all the time. New ideas pop into your head nonstop; the excitement of starting something new overshadows the drudgery of pushing through the hard problems in front of you.

A big difference between Edison (Elon Musk, Phil Knight, [insert other entrepreneurs here] and most start-up founders is that Edison kept going. It's common in the start-up world to hear the phrase, "I'm the idea guy (or gal)!" But in Thomas Edison's case, he was both the idea *and* the execution guy. I'm sure you've heard that it took over one thousand tries to invent the light bulb, but the truth is it took 2,774 attempts to invent the *commercially viable* light bulb. Joseph

Swan, an Englishman, received a patent in the UK for the invention of carbonized paper filaments arcing in a glass lamp in 1878. Swan and Edison would eventually join forces to create Edison-Swan United (commonly known as Ediswan) which became the largest lightbulb producer in the world. With the help of Swan, Edison literally brought light to the world. Eventually, with the funding of J.P. Morgan and other wealthy investors of the time, Edison founded a company that is still going strong today called General Electric.

But let's backtrack a bit: Edison's story of how he finally landed on a thin bamboo filament inside a glass vacuum chamber is significant to all of us entrepreneurs. This was not what he started with. In fact, the first patent awarded to Edison was for a carbon filament similar to Joseph Swan's version.

Today light bulbs are so commonplace that they are almost an afterthought. Can you imagine living in a world where the only sources of light were the sun, candles, lamps, or a fire? Visualize yourself in the room when the invention of the lightbulb happened for the first time…a visceral sense of anticipation fills the anxious silence as the inventor draws closer to doing something that has never been done before. Can you see the oblong glass bulb with the carbon rods beginning to heat, start to glow, and then arc to produce electric light for the first time? Then the room fills with cheers as the dim spark dances inside a modern miracle that would change the world. It's amazing and exhilarating.

This unprecedented scene played out at least five or six times around the world: when Joseph Swan demonstrated his bulb in Newcastle, England, at the Newcastle upon Tyne Chemical Society in 1879; when British scientist Warren de la Rue created a more efficient yet more costly version of a platinum filament in 1840; and again in 1802, when Humphry Davy created an arc light based on the work of the original inventor of the voltaic pile (predecessor of the arc light), Alessandro Volta. So why did all of these amazing, exhilarating, monumental moments similar to Mr. Edison's not end up changing the world? Why did names like Volta, Davy, de la Rue, or Swan never reach the prominence of Edison?

The answer is simple: Volta did his experiment and then bounced to another experiment involving electricity and batteries. De la Rue found the platinum too expensive and jumped to building telescopes and celestial photography; he invented the photoheliograph and went back to chemistry, writing papers on electrical discharge through gases. Swan gave up his endeavor for a few years before focusing on vacuum pumps. There was only one of these men that continued to climb the mountain he originally set out to summit: Thomas Edison. All these entrepreneurs were brilliant, well-educated, well-connected, and richly funded, and had a high degree of social status and access to resources. But only one man brought light to the world. Instead of chasing quick dollars, Edison chased a dream. Instead of spinning off tangential businesses or inventions, he focused on one thing: the commercially viable lightbulb. Edison wasn't a victim of opportunity; he didn't chase the next invention or the easy dollar. Instead, he spent years making his way up the mountain because he had the vision to see, and the grit to stay focused on, the top.

Entrepreneurs often start climbing mountains only to catch sight of smaller, easier hills along their way. These diversions, often complete with beautiful and rewarding vistas of their own, can tempt the climber to leave the path they were on. And because the view is pleasant and the path level, it can be tempting to forget about the mountaintop altogether. I've seen companies go from building guitars to exercise boards, or transition from selling travel expeditions to dresses. I did this myself, in fact, when I started an online sheet music company on my way up the Digital and Marketing Agency Mountain.

The other common problem is that as you build something great, others will want you to take your company in a slightly different direction. This is especially easy to do for a services company. If your services look similar, then why not do something outside your wheelhouse as long as it's close to what you are *really* known for? I did this a few times and got burned every time. My first company was a full service digital and marketing agency, but some clients assumed that because we created interactive websites, we could also do in-depth back-end programming. The dollars were really appealing, and so we let ourselves get distracted and jump into something that wasn't exactly our cup of tea. It turned out disastrously. We didn't know how to bid the jobs accurately and ended up losing money. We went over time and didn't perform up to the standards of our reputation. After a couple rounds of losing money and damaging our standing, we came up with the 80/20 rule (no, not the Pareto Rule). Our rule stated that we could only accept a job if it was 80 percent within our wheelhouse and there was 20 percent or less to learn. We kept to this rule no matter how lucrative or exciting a job seemed and never got burned again.

My friend Chris McChesney wrote in *The 4 Disciplines of Execution,* "There will always be more good ideas than there is a capacity to execute." At the moment when you are yearning for a beautiful view instead of the dirt trail in front of you, the temptation will be really strong to veer off course. Richard Branson has the philosophy that "Business opportunities are like buses, there's always another one coming."

Here are some of the effects of chasing after distractions, easy money, or "the next big thing":

- Bifurcated time, focus, money, and energy
- Loss of economies of scale and time-based efficiencies
- Increased risk of errors
- Lack of expertise
- Loss of institutional knowledge
- Loss of passion
- Loss of family life
- Longer work hours
- Priority paralysis
- Amazement at the mediocre
- Slower progress along all paths
- Loss of momentum

- Brand degradation

Most entrepreneurs struggle to keep one idea moving up the mountain. They end up burning time and resources and risk losing sight of the mountain top altogether.

The reason Thomas Edison brought light to the world was because he stayed on the path and never lost sight of the big dream. He took the original patent with the carbon rods and challenged his own concept of what was needed as a filament. He tested thousands of materials, from expensive metals to carbonized facial hair. Eventually he tried a threaded cotton filament and it worked, producing light for an unheard-of fourteen hours.

Edison bounded to the patent office with this discovery. But he didn't stop there. He continued further up the mountain with each new material he tested. His communications circumnavigated the globe and he deployed workers to scour the planet for the most durable heat-resistant material. Edison tested thousands of plant samples, combing the world for the most suitable filament material.[29] A year after his last patent, William Moore, an employee, sent him bamboo from a sacred temple in Kyoto, Japan. Slicing the bamboo into thin strips and turning it from the cellulose form into a carbonized filament resulted in a bulb that burned up to an astonishing 1,200 hours.

One Idea at a Time

Can you imagine if Edison had taken the path of some of his contemporaries and been enthralled by the shiny new thing atop the smaller hill? If he had started bifurcating his time and focus,

---

29   Edison's Lightbulb. (2017, May 19). Retrieved September 12, 2020, from www.fi.edu/history-resources/edisons-lightbulb.

his investors would have backed out and the press would have lost interest. At this point, your entrepreneur ADD might be screaming, "But only doing one thing is so boring!" Well, Edison actually didn't do just one thing; he just did *one thing at a time.*

Use Edison's model of climbing. Reach the first summit and then see the larger summit behind that one and keep climbing up the same mountain range instead of jumping from mountain to mountain. Focus on your product, create sustainable models for producing it, fine-tune your sales and marketing, and then start climbing the next mountain once you've reached the summit of the first.

A Simple Solution

One great way to fight entrepreneur's ADD is to keep a notebook of "Great Ideas." Capture your ideas as the inspiration strikes, then every quarter, pull out the notebook and see which of the ideas are the most valuable to you. Check if you think the ideas are still relevant, do a personal temperature check on each one and determine if you still feel passionate about it. If it does still excite you, keep it and even rank it. If it doesn't excite you or is no longer relevant, scratch it out. Finally, ask yourself: *Have I made it to the top of the mountain I'm already climbing and do any of these ideas help me climb even higher on my current path?* If not, put the notebook on a shelf so you can keep recording ideas until the next quarter. Otherwise, pull the idea out of the notebook and start executing. I called my notebook "The Book of Fourteen" because I would limit my ideas to fourteen. If one outranked another, then it got room in the book; otherwise I would cross it out to make room for the next greatest spark of inspiration. Yes, both this book and my consulting company have been in my "Book of Fourteen" for a few years, and now that I have the appropriate time and space, I get to execute on that vision.

Overcoming Pitfall 13: Laser Focus

- Buy a notebook specifically for storing your other million-dollar-ideas. EntrepreneursParadox.com/Notebook

- Write down all the great ideas and distractions you would love to explore in the future.

- Create a "Distract from the Distractions" plan. Write down how you are going to remain focused on your current million-dollar-idea, including ways to validate your genius without distracting from what you have now.

- Create an execution plan of how you are going to summit the current mountain. Make it clear and exciting so it motivates you to stay focused.

- Set up a written 80/20 rule for your company. Identify what your company is an expert in (80 percent) and what you are willing to learn (20 percent).

- Define clearly which mountains you are not going to climb at this time and which mountains you will climb in the future.

Pitfall 14

Playing the Victim

"Effective people are not problem-minded; they're opportunity-minded. They feed opportunities and starve problems."

—STEPHEN R. COVEY

Henry J. Kaiser framed this saying, "Problems are only opportunities in work clothes." With a little elbow grease, every problem you experience will become your greatest opportunity. The concept of problems as opportunities was illustrated very clearly for me by some of the most amazing entrepreneurs I know: Mike and Mark Patey. I had the good fortune of going to high school with them, and they're the only twins I know personally to graduate as millionaires from a business they started in high school. Their escapades and business ventures could fill an entire book as they've each started multiple successful businesses, own Guinness World Records, and Mark has written a brilliant book called *Addicts and Millionaires* that describes the often misunderstood gift of ADHD and how it can be used to create greatness.

Mark and Mike started their first business in Orem, Utah, when their dad asked them a profound question: "What businesses are missing?" Or in other words, where are the holes you can fill in the business community? These two eager teens grabbed the yellow pages and started flipping page by page, looking through the listings and ads to find a hole they could fill. After hours of scouring the pages, they realized there wasn't a category, let alone a single listing, for "Deck Builders." No one in the entire valley was advertising in the yellow pages for decks. There were builders, construction firms, and general contractors, but no one specialized in building a deck after a home was already built. So the twin brothers got to work. With lots of effort, a few bouts of customer service genius, and some good luck, they started to gain a great reputation. Once they had the formula down for succeeding with decking, the business grew quickly, and they realized that people love to sit on their decks in hot tubs. So they began selling hot tubs as well and became the largest hot tub retailer in the Western United States. Not too long after, a national competitor moved into Utah. Mark and Mike didn't have the same resources as this behemoth but had ten times more grit.

They went to the drawing board to figure out how to compete with this company, deciding they would have a major parking lot sale. They started telling all their customers and made signs for their retail location. Everything seemed to be going well until one day on the drive home, Mark heard a radio ad for the biggest hot tub sale the state of Utah had ever seen…and it was the same weekend as their sale. To make matters worse, it was only three days away. That meant there was no time to pivot or buy new ads. It seemed like they were going to get their hats handed to them by their aggressive new competitor.

At this point, many would throw their hands in the air and give up. Not the Patey brothers. Instead, they asked, "What do we have to work with here?" They laid out all the variables and discovered that their biggest threat was actually their biggest opportunity. They didn't have the same marketing budget as this national manufacturer, and so they couldn't compete dollar for dollar. Then they realized they didn't have to—they could turn the whole thing on its head and tap into the dollars already being spent. They wrote down the address of where the giant parking lot sale would be and scouted out the location.

There was a big-box retailer with an enormous and partially empty parking lot directly across the street from their competitor's sale. With a little negotiating with the manager, the brothers rented the front half of the parking lot for the coming weekend.

They worked Friday night and into the early morning hours, transporting their hot tubs and getting everything set up. As the sun rose the next morning, the competitor arrived to see another sale happening across the street—one with bigger signs and balloons floating higher in the air. The radio ads ran incessantly that morning and customers streamed in from all over the state, turning into the Pateys' parking lot. The Patey brothers not only outsold their competition, but they sold every hot tub in their inventory.

Every time I think of this story, I smile because the Patey brothers didn't play the victim card and throw in the towel. These boys took a look at the truth of the situation and got excited instead of worried and stressed. They assessed what was in their control and took charge of those things.

The ground is simply an obstacle between the man standing on it and the diamonds beneath. All it takes is the grit to turn it over and dig through the muck until you find them.

Mark and Mike doubled down on solving a seemingly hopeless problem and succeeded wildly. True greatness in entrepreneurship happens when you make the choice to do what others won't, so you can achieve what others can't.

No Excuses

Mark and Mike didn't waste time making excuses. This principle was taught to me powerfully because of an experience on the final approach of Mt. Kilimanjaro. We woke at midnight after a twenty-mile hike and three hours of sleep at base camp. Despite having little rest, we were excited at the prospect of reaching our destination. The temperature had dropped from the eighty-two degrees hiking through the lower two climate zones (Cultivation Zone and Tropical Rainforest) to the mid-twenties of the Arctic Tundra (or Glacial) zone. But that was after the sun had risen and without calculating wind chill. We pulled on our heavy winter gear at a numbing negative four degrees and strapped on our headlamps. Each of us carried a small day pack with water, nutrition, and a couple of emergency items. The final push from Kibo Hut started at 15,430 feet, higher than any mountain in my home state of Utah. Cold and tired, and surrounded by the dark and thin mountain air, there was one last push to the summit. We pulled out our trekking poles and moved them to the rhythmic chants of "Po-le, Po-le" as we started making our way to the top.

At first, no one spoke. The darkness and cold seeped through our clothes and into our souls. It was a very somber mile of switchbacks on the large gravel-like skree. The distance was short at 2.86 miles (4.6 km) but required us to scale nearly 4,000 feet to reach Uhuru Peak. All the mountain climbers and mountain bikers reading this will be trying to calculate the feet per mile at this point, so let me help: it's 1,367 feet per mile with the majority of the 4,000 feet happening in the last two miles, or about two thousand feet per mile. We put one foot in front of the other as we progressed upward, switchback after switchback. In the thinning air, every step seemed to require a full breath: step, breathe, step, breathe, step, breathe. You can see the elevation of those last two miles in the graph below:

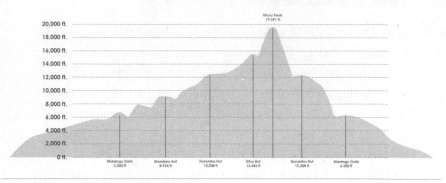

MT. KILIMANJARO ELEVATION CHART

With heads pounding and hearts pumping, our group of fourteen hikers (and as many guides) made it to a small icy cave that provided us momentary shelter from the blustery wind. Simon, our main guide for this portion of the trek, announced, "We only rest five minutes. Then we go." Several people sat and, it seemed as though when they dropped to the cave floor, their morale dropped with them. Some began to grumble about not being able to make it to the top. When Simon said it was time to go, several people requested another five minutes and others admitted they didn't think they could make it any further, knowing the difficulty of traversing back down the mountain.

We checked each other for signs of hypoxia and shared supplements and support. Even offering words of encouragement in the thin air was hard. After another five minutes of trying to lift people's spirits, we offered a hand and lifted them physically to their feet and out of the cave. Once again, the darkness wrapped its icy fingers around us and began to squeeze.

Nary a word was spoken as we trudged like well-outfitted zombies up the mountain. After a while, I realized it was so steep that there were switchbacks inside of switchbacks. The physical exhaustion was real, but at this point the mental exhaustion was the greater challenge. Then, as the earth and air grew even colder and fatigue threatened to break us completely, this happened:

The sun rose behind the opposing summit, Mawenzi Peak, gilding the earth in a bath of resplendent light and life. As soon as we saw the luminous beauty above the distant terrain, we were filled with warmth…energy…hope…gratitude…and light. Not a single eye was left dry at the splendor and magnificence of this gift. The sunrise broke so gently above the curvature of the earth, the change was almost imperceptible. At first, it was nothing more than a slit in the darkness along the curved horizon which created the slightest gradient distinction between earth and sky. It pushed powerfully yet silently upward until it broke the plane of the skyline, when the shades of darkness became glorious life-bringing hues of amber and gold. Once the celestial body peeked above the edge of the earth, light burst open the former reality of night and filled it with the dawn. Having the sun join us on our journey renewed our spirits and replenished our strength. The pressing weight of the darkness had been lifted as we marched toward a destination that no longer seemed so far away. We expected the sun to illuminate the summit above. And it did. What we didn't expect was who this newfound light revealed on the trail in front of us.

With the sun first floating over Mawenzi at 6:34 a.m., we saw something I never expected. There ahead of us was another group conquering this goliath in a very different way. We had been hiking for five and a half hours when the sun pulled back the curtain of darkness, and there before us was another group that must have been above us the whole time and may have been pushing for the summit twice as long. This group was part of an organization called Paratrek—a collection of amazing people who had climbed the same mountain we were climbing in the same freezing temperatures with the same elevation and same lack of oxygen, but without full use of their legs. They were using canes, crutches, and even wheelchairs to make it to the top of the mountain! I couldn't believe what I was seeing.

I sat down with one of these heroes and was nearly overwhelmed with emotions. Through my heavy breathing, I managed to ask, "What possessed you to do this superhuman feat?"

"Why wouldn't I?" came his simple reply. The response was instant and powerful. There was no room for a victim mindset in his words.

It didn't matter that he had to climb the mountain differently; he could still climb.

It didn't matter that his legs didn't work like everyone else's; they still worked.

It didn't matter that it took significantly more effort to climb; he had effort to give.

It didn't matter that he had crippled limbs; his heart was strong.

It didn't matter that it took twice as long; he made it to the top.

A look of amazement was still on my face as the man explained further: "I used to play the victim and thought about all the things I couldn't do. One day I was sick of thinking about my limitations and started thinking about what I was capable of." He pointed up the mountain and said, "…and I'm capable of this."

I hugged him and thanked him for changing me forever that day. Who was I to complain about tired legs and sore feet ever again?

And so, I pose this question to you: are you going to make excuses or make it to the top of the mountain? The mountain is there; the choice is yours.

Finding Serenity above the Storm

Long before I climbed Mt. Kilimanjaro, I was a young high school kid who loved to ski but didn't always have the money to do so. My friend Gavin and I purchased tickets to Solitude Resort and Saturday morning we were some of the first skiers ready to jump on the lift. That morning, right before the chairs started moving up the mountain, a storm rolled in and hit us hard. "Storm" may be too mild of a word as this was a full-on blizzard.

Because of my shortage of cash and the no-refund policy at the
resort, Gavin and I decided to embark up the mountain anyway. As
others were taking off their skis and getting back in their cars, Gavin
and I frigidly braved the maelstrom. It dumped so much snow that
we could barely see the next chair as the lift glided up to the top of
the mountain.

About three-quarters of the way up, we broke out of the clouds to
discover a bright and sunny day. Instead of a storm, we found acres
of fresh powder laid peacefully on the mountain; and we had it all
to ourselves. In the valley, and even at the base of the mountain, the
snowfall was intense. But we did what no one else was willing to do—
we chose to continue up. The reward was the softest virgin powder
we'd ever experienced. And save for maybe three others, we had the
entire mountain to ourselves while snow pummeled the valley below.

So, how do you tap into the excitement to go where no one else has
gone? To see what no one else will ever see? How do you gather
the courage to be excited for the next impossible situation? All you
have to do is change a few words and you will change the way you
see the world. You will even change what happens inside your body,

physiologically. Allison Wood Brooks proved the effectiveness of changing language in a study done at Harvard University, which we will discuss further later in this chapter.

A good friend of mine, Jesse Sitterud, shared with me something that has profoundly affected my life and changed the way I see stressful situations. He said, "Life doesn't happen to you, it happens for you." Every day is a new opportunity to grow. Life doesn't actually have problems; it only has challenges to overcome—exciting challenges.

If starting a business were easy, everyone would do it. The beauty is in the fact that it is hard. Hard means only a few will accept the challenge. Only a small group of people will see the challenges as exciting opportunities to do something great. The harder it is, the fewer will attempt it and the more opportunity for you (just like the few who braved the weather on the slopes that day to find the prize waiting above). Also, the harder it is, the better the story when it's all over. Have you ever seen a movie about someone doing something easy and mundane? Think about the percentage of movies that tell the stories of war heroes, athletes, lawyers, knights, astronauts, or superheroes. We enjoy watching the protagonist overcome something seemingly insurmountable. The more of a challenge presented, the greater the reward when it's conquered. Those who take the greatest risks reap the greatest rewards.

Eustress Versus Distress

In most cultures, we think of stress as a bad thing. But there are two very different types of stress: eustress and distress (similar to euphoria and dysphoria). Eustress is viewed as a positive emotional state and is accompanied by enthusiasm and feelings of fulfillment and arousal. It typically increases focus, enhances performance, and boosts skill level. This is commonly called excitement. Distress is viewed as a negative emotional state and can lead to anxiety and panic. Under distress, the brain can't think clearly, and performance is decreased.

It is fascinating to look at the body's physiological response to both anxiety (distress) and excitement (eustress). In a state of stress, the human body experiences the following physiological changes:

- Rapid heart rate

- Stronger contractions of the heart

- Increase in blood pressure

- Release of stress hormones

  - Adrenaline (triggers heart and lungs to engorge and produce "super" strength or speed)

  - Noradrenaline

  - Cortisol

  - Endorphins (mask pain by blocking nerve impulses)

- Change in breathing

- Glucose (sugar) levels increase

- Digestive activity declines (as blood supply is redirected to vital organs)

- Hypervigilance

- Sweating

Consider a few differences between distress and eustress.

Physiological Change	Distress (Anxiety)	Eustress (Excitement)
Nucleus accumbens in the brain's limbic system	Dormant	Activates and provides "reward" chemicals, dopamine and serotonin, to the body
Blood vessels	Over 175 bpm vasoconstriction (constricting of the blood vessels) occurs constricting the blood vessels and depriving the muscles of oxygen	Blood vessels dilate, increasing the flow of blood to muscles
Pupils	Tunnel vision can occur due to increased levels of adrenaline produced by high anxiety	Visual acuity is enhanced, and performance increases
Ears	Auditory exclusion	Enhanced auditory cognition
Brain	Sensory overload (freezing)	Intuitive decision-making
Emotional state	Driven by fear	Driven by desire

These are some subtle yet critical physiological differences. The biggest difference is the activation of the nucleus accumbens when feeling excitement. The nucleus accumbens is the pleasure/reward center of the limbic system; it provides dopamine and serotonin which have the effect of satiety.[30] [31] When you are excited, you have almost all of the same physiological changes as stress, but your brain is saying you'll be rewarded for this experience. The nucleus accumbens doesn't work alone; it partners with the ventral tegmental area and works closely with the prefrontal cortex—both of which increase the pleasure and reward response. Working with the prefrontal cortex increases decision-making ability and helps hyper focus. This is not the case with fear that comes from anxiety. There

30   Predictable Fear. (2014, October 31). Retrieved September 22, 2020, from www.psychologytoday.com/us/blog/prefrontal-nudity/201410/predictable-fear.

31   Klucken, T., Tabbert, K., Schweckendiek, J., Merz, C. J., Kagerer, S., Vaitl, D., & Stark, R. (2009). Contingency learning in human fear conditioning involves the ventral striatum. Human Brain Mapping, 30(11), 3636-3644. doi:10.1002/hbm.20791.

is no reward center activation. There is only a feeling of dread and impending doom.

Distress and eustress are both aroused emotions. Your brain is priming the body for action. One type of action is fight-or-flight; but another is what I've entitled **Thrill-and-Skill**.

Fight-or-Flight vs. Thrill-and-Skill

Fight-or-flight is driven by fear and self-preservation. Thrill-and-skill is driven by desire. The thrill part is your nucleus accumbens squirting dopamine and serotonin into your body. You become "thrilled"about the high-risk activity you're about to perform. The skill part means that your body and brain are becoming physiologically more adept at difficult tasks because of all the cardiovascular, circulatory, muscular, endocrine, and central nervous system changes.

Change Your Language to Change Your Brain

Think about the last time you felt stressed. There is a good chance that either you or a friend said, "Try and relax." In a 2013 study performed by Alison Wood Brooks of the Harvard Business School, she found that 84.94 percent of participants gave themselves the advice of "try to relax or calm down." In the study, she cites this as the antithesis of how to deal with stress. She cites the WWII British slogan, "Keep Calm and Carry On" as an ineffective way to reduce or reframe anxiety. Both distress and excitement are *aroused* emotions that change the body physiologically in almost the exact same way. The two emotions are "arousal congruent."

Alison wanted to see if her hypothesis of changing our language to change our outcome was possible. In the first of three experiments, she asked participants to sing in front of others. Before the performance, she randomly assigned each person one of three statements to recite out loud, "I am anxious," "I am excited," or no statement. Those who verbally stated "I am excited" reported feeling more excited. Although the feeling is an important measure, the more objective metric of singing accuracy was found highest in the group that verbalized, "I am excited," at 80.52 percent. They used software to measure the accuracy of the singer's pitch on a well-known song. The "no statement" group was significantly lower at 69.27 percent accuracy, and the "I am anxious" group hit the bottom of the ranks at 52.98 percent. Self-efficacy was also much higher when those three words were uttered, meaning each participant was significantly more confident in their ability to execute. Overall, the participants felt positive about the experience, were more confident in their ability, and had a significantly better performance by simply pronouncing the words, "I am excited." She repeated the experiment with public speaking and solving math problems (two inherently stressful situations) and derived the same results. Those who changed their thinking by changing their speech performed better, felt happier, enjoyed the experience more, and had more confidence in their abilities.

In several other studies, one of the overriding emotions that differentiate eustress and distress is the feeling of control and being able to handle a given situation. When we are anxious, it feels like the situation is outside of our control and beyond our ability to cope or affect the outcome. When we are excited, we take a look at what we do have the ability to affect and change within our own power.

Whatever your insurmountable challenge is, take two minutes and write it down with the following phrasing:

I am excited about _____.

For example, in the case of Mark and Mike, they would have said something like:

"I am excited about finding a way to beat our competitor this weekend."

Here are some other statements that can be reappraised as exciting challenges rather than insurmountable problems:

- *Our retention rate stinks **vs.** I am excited to win back our customers.*

- *I can't make payroll **vs.** I am excited to figure out how to make payroll.*

- *The website is broken again **vs.** I am excited to fix our website.*

- *Our expenses keep outpacing our revenue **vs.** I am excited to create a viable budget.*

- *We keep running out of money **vs.** I am excited to figure out cash flow.*

- *Our product isn't as good as our competitor's **vs.** I am excited to develop the best product on the planet.*

- *Things keep changing and we can't keep up **vs.** I am excited to adapt and thrive.*

- *We keep falling behind in our shipments **vs.** I am excited to keep up with demand.*

- *We can't get the parts we need when we need them **vs.** I am excited to figure out a viable sourcing model for our product.*

- *We keep messing up **vs.** I am excited to plug the holes in our company.*

Because language is so powerful, let's dissect these statements. The ones on the left are mostly victim statements. They are negative and feel depressing and present as statements of fact when they are really just distortion. They also have no action tied to them; they feel beyond control and beyond the ability to cope. In contrast, the excitement statements on the right are exactly that—exciting and full of hope. They live in the present and tap into individual power. They are action statements containing a verb that moves toward progress. They are within your personal power to affect.

Learning to turn problems into opportunities is really about a choice between extremes: to see yourself as the victim or the opportunist; to fear the storm or look for what lies beyond; to steer stress toward a positive emotional driver or succumb to its limits; to employ the language of excitement or that of anxiousness. That choice, because it is individual and completely up to you, is within the power of every entrepreneur who is not only enticed by beginning their journey, but wants to marshal the strength to see it all the way through to the end.

Overcoming Pitfall 14: Get Excited About Challenges

- Write down your five biggest challenges.

- Rewrite your five biggest challenges as excitement statements.

- Recite these statements out loud every morning as part of your "Power Hour."

- Reflect on your emotional state when you read them and how different it feels.

- Set an appointment in your calendar at the beginning of the week to look at the new set of challenges.

- Share your excitement statements and be featured on our website at EntrepreneursParadox.com/Excited.

Pitfall 15

Lacking Structure

A solid foundation determines whether buildings tumble or continue standing after an earthquake.

An essential part of mountaineering is understanding the supportive structure of the ice beneath you. For example, on Mt. Everest, many climbers choose their route based on the stability and predictability of the ice that will be underfoot. In the same way, an entrepreneur must rely on the structure of their business as a means to help them up the mountain, or if the structure is faulty, unstable, or weak, this can actually result in dire consequences and bring the climb to a sudden and even disastrous result. Unlike the mountain, however, entrepreneurs have control over the metaphorical ice that can provide a sure foundation for the climb ahead. There are four important components to your corporate structure that will help you succeed in building your business and making the summit:

- Ownership Structure
- Leadership Structure
- Legal Structure
- Board Structure

Ownership Structure

Don't give away the farm. In fact, don't even give away the pigs.

Every company is controlled by its owners. In most startups, there is a majority shareholder: you, the founder. In some cases, dilution has already happened, and the company has multiple owners. Hopefully, this is not you. If it is, I hope you've kept the large majority of the ownership. This is not a greedy tactic. Yes, ownership does equate to dollars on the back end, but it also determines who has the final say on key decisions. Having someone at the top who is understood as the final decision-maker is critical to the speed of doing business as a start-up.

A common mistake I see a lot of entrepreneurs make (myself included) is to give away the company percentage by percentage. This immediately creates legal and logistical issues until there is not enough ownership left to make the company worth pursuing. One founder I worked with gave 25 percent to two of the first people he brought in, leaving them collectively with 50 percent and him with 50 percent. This created a deadlock because, collectively, the two new owners had as much ownership as the original founder. It's common for founders to give ownership to important employees, and at times to investors. Either way, the principle remains the same. You, as the founder and leader of the company, need to maintain control long-term. At the beginning of the book we talked about which mountain you were going to climb and the duration you'd be climbing. You need to maintain majority ownership until you hit your goal and plant your flag on the summit.

Many people go into business with a partner and think it is a good idea to split the ownership 50/50. That seems fair, right? Splitting ownership might be a great idea at the start and you might get along wonderfully in the beginning, but the fact is people, their situations, and motivations change. What is great today may not be so great tomorrow. I have yet to see a successful long-term 50/50 co-ownership relationship work. Many leadership teams change within one to two years. There needs to be a single leader, and that leader needs to be you. A 51/49 split takes the ambiguity out of decision-making, despite giving a lion's share of the company away (which isn't something I'd ever recommend anyway).

Maintaining decision-making control means that you plan how you are going to distribute ownership over the entire duration of your company from formation through end goal. A founder might really depend on the two employees to help grow the business in the beginning, but what happens when the third "critical employee" comes along? Does the founder give up more shares? The best scenario is all three of the new owners give up shares in proportion to their ownership, so it dilutes everyone. Otherwise the new owners have as much voting power as the original founder, and they may not agree to diluting their shares.

Plan for if and when you want to divide ownership, but as I advised earlier, don't give away the farm. There are so many ways to provide key employees ownership. I won't go into all of them but rather offer some guidelines and points to consider.

Offering Ownership Is a Taxable Event

One thing that is often overlooked in giving/gifting ownership is that the event is taxable. If someone is offered ownership without paying for it, they will be taxed for the full amount. That's why vesting is a good idea: it spreads out the gain and spreads out the tax burden.

Build a "Top of the Mountain" Org Chart

Plan out what your company org chart will look like when you hit your goal. Consider the key roles you'd likely give ownership to, and only plan to give away ownership as a last resort. There are so many other incentives you can provide to key employees like bonuses, rewards, incentive plans, commissions, etc. Either way, you're best served when you have a roadmap for how (and if) you'll use ownership as an incentive, how it will best serve the long-term goals of the organization, and how to resist the temptation of giving too much away, too early, and to the wrong individuals at the wrong time.

Use Vesting and Employee Stock Options

If you do decide to give away ownership as part of your growth plan, consider using vesting or reverse vesting and employee stock options. Vesting and reverse vesting means you give someone units/ shares which become available to them over time. These are set up as a way for your fellow leaders to earn their ownership and can be tied to performance, goals, or simply time. Whatever the trigger, all vesting schedules have a time component, meaning the key employee is awarded ownership over time. If the employee sees the company through to the top of the mountain, then they are rewarded with more and more ownership. The more effort and time, the more ownership. One provision you'll want to include for employees is if there is an equity event earlier than the designated timing for reaching the goal, then all of their shares will vest immediately at the time of transaction.

Create a Capitalization Table

Make sure there is enough ownership for you as the founder all the way to the goal. Consider the following example of a simple cap table (capitalization table) for a company with one million shares. Note how this chart reflects the end goal in mind:

Shareholder	Common (voting) Shares	Common Nonvoting	Preferred (nonvoting)	Options	Total	%	Vesting Period
Founder	700,000	0	0	0	700,000	70%	0
COO	60,000	0	0	0	60,000	6%	3 years
CFO	60,000	0	0	0	60,000	6%	3 years
CTO	60,000	0	0	0	60,000	6%	4 years
VP Sales	0	35,000	0	0	35,000	4%	5 years
VP Marketing	0	35,000	0	0	35,000	4%	5 years
Director 1	0	0	0	10,000	10,000	1%	3 Years
Director 2	0	0	0	5,000	5,000	1%	3 Years
Director 3	0	0	0	5,000	5,000	1%	3 Years
Other Employees	0	0	0	30,000	30,000	3%	5 Years
Total	880,000	70000	0	50000	1,000,000	100%	

(Note: This chart is strictly for example purposes and is not a guide for what to give individual contributors.)

The "Preferred" column is all zeros because at this point no investment dollars have been put into the company. Preferred shares typically have no voting rights, but they are the first to be paid and usually have a regularly scheduled dividend attached to them. Also notice that, in the example, there are only four voting members. These are the people in the company that will have a say on major decisions like an equity event, merger or acquisition, capital raise, going public, dissolution, and other big decisions. All shareholders will profit from an equity event and, based on the way it's set up, can benefit from distributions.

The column entitled "Options" is for employees who would like to own part of the company. They have the *option* to buy into ownership, and it's a great idea to provide an employee stock option plan. This gives employees the ability to become part of the company if they elect to purchase their options when they vest. Options are technically not "given" and a change in ownership of options is a nontaxable event. Gifting ownership to employees *is* a taxable event and will need to be reported to the tax service in your country.

Determine a Distribution Structure

Now that ownership is decided, it's a good idea to determine a distribution structure. Distributions are typically determined on profits and are distributed quarterly. This is flexible and can be given out whenever the company deems it wise, but having a regular cadence and set criteria to evaluate the feasibility eliminates a lot of strife. Having this determined beforehand makes things a lot easier. A great structure is to look at profits quarterly and set performance goals as guidelines for distributions. If the goals are met, then the profits are distributed. If not, then the money stays in the company.

Leadership Structure

As the founder, you are the leader. This is important to reflect on often, as "decision by committee" is the fastest way to slow a company down. Wanting help to make decisions is commonplace for new entrepreneurs, often stemming from a lack of experience, confidence, or a desire to involve everyone in the decision-making process. Doing so, however, can lead to groupthink and cause strife in a company. There needs to be a single leader with a "the buck stops here" mentality and who is ultimately responsible for the success and failure of the company. As the founder, *you* are the leader until you give that power away. My recommendation is, don't give it away. It's good to have others who have a vote on different matters because they can offer unique perspectives and be a true benefit to the entrepreneur in seeing things beyond their own peripheral vision. As a general rule, remember that each person on your team needs to be empowered to make all decisions for their entire responsibility. The founder/CEO needs to be able to make decisions for the entire company as a whole.

Specify the decision-making authority in advance to save a lot of headaches and eliminate any doubt. For example, determine:

- Who can make financial decisions and in what dollar amounts?

- Who has signing authority?

- Who can hire and fire?

- Who can change organizational structure?

One of the decisions I regret the most was due to not specifying who had financial authority and at what level. I had a VP who was one of the most loyal men I have ever known, but he made an independent financial decision and I let him go because of it. In retrospect, I can now see he was trying to help the company by giving out employee bonuses for some really hard-working programmers. At the time, however, I was stressed about finances and made a quick decision to let him go. The reality was that I had not set the guidelines in advance for this type of action. He has since graciously forgiven me, and I count him as one of my greatest friends. This all could have been avoided, however, if there were clear guidelines in place for specifying who had financial and signing authority and in what amounts. Once you have all the guidelines in place, having clear boundaries makes everyone's lives a lot easier.

As the founder, I would also suggest you maintain the title of CEO. This is more than just a cool name; a C-level title usually has a seat on the board and is organizationally over the rest of the C-level positions. "President" is a great title, but it is not inherently a board position. I've seen some entrepreneurs put the title of "Founder / CEO / President" on their business cards because I assume they want recognition or control. But keep in mind that it's the CEO title that's important for decision-making. If and when you dive into the investment world, investors will want to know who the CEO is.

For key individuals in the company (major shareholders) it's a good idea to acquire Key Person insurance to provide a safety net in case someone passes away. The purpose of Key Person insurance is to infuse the company with cash to help the organization keep growing even in the tough situation of someone's passing. It is calculated from percentage of ownership and role in the company.

Legal Structure

When starting a business, the legal entity is important. As an individual, you can form a sole proprietorship. With a partner, you can form a partnership. The biggest reason you don't want to be either of these entities is because of liability. With both a sole proprietorship and partnership, you are completely vulnerable and liable for any legal action. Forming a corporation protects you from these risks and is even articulated in the name of an LLC: Limited Liability Corporation. Think back to your goals and the three paths: if your end goal is to get investment / buy or be bought, you will need to be a corporation because it also limits the risk for the investment

group. If you are looking to go public someday, the transition from
S-Corp to C-Corp is the easiest (a C-Corp is for large companies like
IBM and General Motors). If you are looking for legal protection
and rapid growth without the hassle of all the regulations, then LLC
is your path. Spend the time and engage the services of a lawyer to
become a corporation.

The following table describes the differences and benefits to each type
of legal formation:

	LLC	S-Corp
Mandatory year-end shareholders meeting	No	Yes
Pass through income for taxes	Yes	Yes
Number of members	Unlimited	100
Pretax expense deductions (phones, uniforms, travel, computers, etc.)	Yes	Yes
Cost to start	$1,000s	$1,000s
Flexible salary structure	Yes	No
All shareholders must be US citizens	No	Yes
Multiple classes of units/stock	Yes	No
Potential additional state taxes	No	Yes
Best path to going public and becoming C-Corp	No	Yes
Owners must be individuals, not companies	No	Yes
Can be owned by other corporations	Yes	No
Can be owned by investment groups	Yes	No
Can be owned by trusts and estates	Yes	Yes
Decreased paperwork	Yes	No

	LLC	S-Corp
Federally recognized entity by the IRS	No	Yes
Voting and nonvoting ownership	Yes	Yes
Type of ownership	Units	Shares
Forced to transition to C-Corp if requirements are not met	No	Yes
Easier to expand rapidly	Yes	No
Business profits are reported on personal tax returns	Yes	No
Profits are reported on the company tax return	No	Yes
Expiration	Perpetual	Perpetual
Mandatory board of directors	No	Yes

As you can see, there are many more restrictions, rules, and procedures for an S-Corp versus an LLC. The biggest reason to form an S-Corp is for tax benefits, although LLCs still have some great tax benefits of their own. In an S-Corp, the profits are taxed to the business, so the owners are not responsible personally for out-of-pocket taxes. An important question to ask yourself at this point is, what type of growth are you committed to? If you are truly committed to rapid growth, an S-Corp is probably not for you. Rapid growth comes with a need for capital infusions. If the company is formed as an S-Corp, these infusions can't come from outside investment groups—only individuals, debt financing, or reinvestment of current members. Reinvestment into the company eliminates some of the tax advantage of an S-Corp. Rapid expenses means write-off on taxes. An LLC that can show a loss each year (think added expenses due to growth) will have zero tax burden on the owners and can result in a tax return in most cases. In deciding between an S-Corp and LLC, the question you need to ask is whether the additional time, regulations, and expenses are worth it in your business right now. I suggest forming an LLC for most of my clients. For a quick reference point, go to the website and use the business entity calculator found at EntrepreneursParadox.com/Entity

Once you've decided what entity to organize, you will need to create a solid Operating Agreement (LLC) or Corporate Bylaws (S-Corp). This agreement is necessary to the business running smoothly and for avoiding conflict so the business can grow rapidly. A solid agreement is the foundation for how important decisions are made in the company. This document will be filed with the state you are located in and sets out all the governance, rights, and responsibilities of the members that hold an ownership interest. Make sure your agreement contains the following:

- **Ownership Interest**
  A cap table is an important part of the agreement, so everyone is clear on how the organization ownership is distributed.

- **Rights and Responsibilities of Members and Managers**
  Members are owners, Managers are decision makers and day-to-day operators.

- **Structure for Profits and Losses Distribution**
  Define ahead of time the rules for when and how to take distributions.

- **Voting Rules**
  Outline who has voting rights in what percentages and how votes are organized.

- **Rules for Making Big Decisions**
  Understand what constitutes a majority or supermajority; spell out each of the decisions and the voting percentage needed to ratify these decisions.

- **Ownership Changes**
  This is a big one. Make sure you have clearly defined rules for changing ownership including: buying, selling, gifting, or the unfortunate event of a death.

- **Dissolution Rules**
  Determine how the company will wind down if necessary. How is dissolution voted on? How are assets distributed? Who is responsible for closing the books? What is the order of priority in liquidation?

- **Fiscal Year**
  Corporations don't have to adhere to a calendar year. I highly advise that you do. It makes everything simpler. At this stage of the game, you most likely don't need a different fiscal year.

- **Board Structure**
  Clearly delineate the number of board members, what the board votes on, what the board doesn't vote on, when the board convenes, fiduciary duties, payment, and how board meetings are to be handled. This is a requirement for S-Corps. For LLCs, I suggest starting with a nonfiduciary advisory board rather than a formal board of directors.

Lastly, make sure you have an employment agreement that is rock solid. Some founders skip this step because it is just them or them and their partner. Shareholders/owners are not guaranteed to be employees, and owners can work at the company or not. These details need to be distinguished in an employment agreement. For the good of the company, this agreement needs a bulletproof Confidentiality or Non-Disclosure Agreement (NDA), Non-Compete, Non-Solicitation, and Technology Privacy provisions. Other important pieces of the agreement include job title, compensation, benefits and premiums, bonuses (different from distributions), termination procedure, and performance expectations.

Board Structure

For an S-Corp, it is a requirement to have a board of directors. For an LLC, it is a good idea to have an advisory board. Either way, the selection process is important. A board serves an important function and can be a huge boon to the company, especially in rapid growth mode. Select an odd number of board members to prevent deadlocks in voting.

> Fiduciary: A person or organization that manages money, assets, or property on behalf of another with the responsibility to put the other person's interests above their own. A fiduciary is bound legally and ethically to perform these duties.

The most important part of board selection is to align your board with your vision and the mountain you've decided to climb. Select a diverse board; according to the SEC (Securities and Exchange Commission), there is a strong correlation between having a diverse board and the financial performance of a company. They share that "companies with a high ratio of diverse board seats exceeded the average returns of the Dow Jones and NASDAQ indices over a five-year period."[32] Start by assigning seats by skill sets, then try to find diverse people to fill those seats. Don't recruit all lawyers, all people in your industry, or all accountants. You really want to find a mix of experiences. Next, look at cultural, experiential, and educational backgrounds to offer varied perspectives on the company and its path toward growth. Don't be afraid to bring on people of different ages, geographies, gender, or race. Remember that the purpose of the board is to question everything you do and connect you to people and opportunities that will help you rapidly grow.

If you have a homogenous board, you will get a lot more groupthink and will not be able to grow as fast. Regardless of who you bring on to the board, find critical thinkers, strategic planners, and problem solvers who are well-connected. Board member connections are a key component to outside growth, hiring, and future investment. Again, you want diversity in networks as well. If everyone on your board runs in the same circles, then you will benefit less from having ties to groups you wouldn't otherwise know.

The final component which is a must for board members is a high emotional quotient (often defined as emotional intelligence with a high degree of empathy). The last thing you want for your board is hours of arguing. I've seen volatile boards and it is counterproductive. Make sure your board members have the skills and the wisdom to know how to help you in a centered way. Here are the skill sets I suggest for filling seats on your board:

- Industry Expertise (one or two seats)

- Business Model Competence (in a different industry)

- Legal

- Financial/Investment

---

32 Speech by SEC Commissioner: Diversity in the Boardroom Yields Dividends. (2009, September 10). Retrieved September 12, 2020, from www.sec.gov/news/speech/2009/spch091009laa.htm.

- Strategic

- Management/Operations

- Marketing

- Sales

Building a robust structure for your organization may not be the most glamorous of activities, but it provides the support and framework to withstand the journey up the entrepreneurial mountain. When the ownership, leadership, legal, and board structures are thought out in advance and built with the end in mind, it furthers the likelihood of success.

Overcoming Pitfall 15: Build a Solid Foundation

- With a mentor or coach, write out the cap table of where you will be when you reach your summit. Include key employees and an options pool.

- Go to the website and use the business structure calculator to determine which type of business entity is right for you.

- Call your lawyer and create or review the structural documents for your company, including:

  - Articles of Organization

  - Operating Agreement (LLC)/By-Laws (S-Corp)

  - Employment Agreement

- Identify which roles and how many seats you want on your board.

- Write a list of all the people you know who could fill those roles.

- Go to LinkedIn and check their number of connections (the bigger the better).

- While on LinkedIn, check how much overlap these potential board members have with each other.

- Give them a call and invite them to your board.

- Schedule a quarterly board meeting (make sure to have great food).

Get access to a sample Operating Agreement[33] at EntrepreneursParadox.com/OA

Want to find out which entity suits you best? Go to the website and use the business entity calculator found at EntrepreneursParadox.com/Entity

---

33   *You will need to review it with your lawyer before officially filing.

Pitfall 16

Losing Sight of Culture

Great company culture can be defined as a shared group passion toward a goal.

You may not realize this, but you already have a corporate culture in place. And like it or not, it's *you*. It's kind of like the old family saying: "If Momma ain't happy, ain't nobody happy." Your actions and attitudes determine the tone and mood of the company. What you believe, the vision you share, and how you act will be adopted as the culture. I love the TV show *Undercover Boss* because CEOs go to the front lines of their companies and find cultural issues they didn't imagine or intend, only later to realize it most likely started with them.

Since you are the guidepost for your company culture, consider what tenets you can use to have a work environment that will produce the highest results and the happiest employees. What kind of environment would you like to work in if you weren't the boss? Are there companies you've worked for in the past that had an environment you loved being in? This is a good place to start, but it's important to understand what culture is and what it isn't.

The Meaning of Culture

Forbes, Inc., and *Fortune Magazine* publish annual lists ranking the best places to work. They cite factors such as competitive pay, maternity and paternity leave, free meals for employees, foosball tables, unlimited PTO, and pet insurance. This can easily be misunderstood as company culture when it's really not. The definition of culture is "the set of shared attitudes, values, goals, and practices that characterizes an institution or organization."[34]

Culture is much more than "the things" a company has. I've known companies with foosball tables, free meals, and even yoga studios, yet the employees reported they had a horrible culture—the foosball tables sat unplayed, people were scared to use their unlimited PTO for fear of reprimand, and the free meals meant everyone had to work through lunch. Culture isn't about the Tornado 3,000 tournament foosball table proudly on display, but it is about spending thirty minutes a day laughing and getting to know the people in your company—the very same people who are all working hard to make your vision come true.

Part of the culture we had making it to the top of Kilimanjaro was excitement, curiosity, teamwork, fun, and progression toward our shared goal. We sang, we laughed, we shared stories, and at times we literally lifted each other as we climbed.

One of the greatest examples of a beautiful culture was shown to me by James Ivie. I was working at a start-up called Agilix and we were creating a revolutionary new way to use digital technologies for learning called BrainHoney. I had taken on the responsibility to create and program a fairly complex crossword-puzzle-style game along with all the other things I had on my plate. Work was progressing rapidly, but even with the extended hours I wasn't keeping up with

---

34   Culture. (n.d.). Retrieved September 12, 2020, from www.merriam-webster.com/dictionary/culture.

everything I had to do. The pressure was mounting, and the deadlines were looming. Others in the office could tell my stress levels were rising as the deadlines grew closer. I'm sure some speculation was mounting about my ability to finish all the tasks on my plate. I ended up prioritizing other things over the app and only started working on it the Friday before it was due. Even working all weekend, there just wasn't enough time to get it done.

First thing Monday morning, James walked into my office and asked if he could show me something. We sat down and he pulled up a fully functional version of the crossword puzzle game—the same game I had agreed to build but hadn't finished. There it was, in full splendor. The look of confusion on my face lasted for well over a minute. He said, "I finished my assignments a little early last week and knew how much you had on your plate, so I thought I would see if I could help and take a crack at the game."

Still in utter amazement, I couldn't believe what I was seeing. Befuddled, I asked, "Why did you do this, James? I don't understand."

He responded, "I knew you had a lot on your plate and wanted to help. There are things you can do that I can't, but *this* I could help with."

I wanted a better understanding, so I continued to question him. "But *why*, James? You could have spent your weekend having fun. Why did you help me?"

His response has had a profoundly lasting effect on me to this day: "This is my company too, you know." James didn't have a job; he had a vision. James had ownership and a goal to get to the top of the mountain together. He saw that my pack was loaded down with a few too many items and he willingly took one to carry in his. He didn't say, "Looks like that guy has too much stuff. Oh, well. It may be slowing us down but, hey, it's *his* pack." James was more focused on the bigger vision and getting us all to the top of the mountain than who had more or less than anyone else. His vision transcended his personal space into the vision of what we can become together. A positive culture starts with six aspects: vision/purpose, respect, gratitude, safety, growth, service, and contribution.

Vision and Purpose

There is no expedition without a vision of which mountain to climb. Eleanor Roosevelt said, "The future belongs to those who believe in the beauty of their dreams." Andrew Scivally, the founder and CEO of eLearning Brothers, exemplifies this more than anyone I've ever had the privilege of working with. He believes in the greatness of the mountain and the greatness of everyone climbing to the summit. He sees the difficult road ahead and believes in everyone's abilities to make it to the top. And he sees it in everyone so sincerely that they start to believe in it themselves. Because of this, eLearning Brothers became one of the fastest growing companies in the Silicon Slopes region.

Contribution

Multiple studies have shown that the most desired aspect of any job is the ability to contribute. This comes out on top every time and ranks higher than compensation, perks, or the benefits package. As humans, we have an innate desire to contribute to and make the world a better place. If we can contribute to something great (vision), then the satisfaction will be even that much higher. The best way to accomplish this is to tie the responsibilities of each employee to the company vision and then see how they can contribute. Make sure each employee is empowered to make contributions, and then clear the path so they can contribute most effectively. Disney does an amazing job of empowering their Cast Members at the park to contribute and make a difference. One hot vacation day, my one-year-old daughter had an explosion in (and out of) her diaper. It was a mess. A very sweet employee passing by saw the incident and immediately ran over to assist. She literally helped clean my daughter up and then escorted us into a gift shop, pulled a onesie off the shelf, gave it to us free of charge, and wished us a happy day. She was empowered to make these decisions by the leadership team. That employee transformed a potentially rotten experience into an amazing day not to be forgotten. Let your team contribute and make sure they know what effect it has toward achieving the overall goal.

Safety

When we mention cultural safety, we're not talking about OSHA requirements. We're referencing emotional safety, which includes feeling stable in one's position with the company and feeling safe with the day-to-day activities and responsibilities of the job. In the beginning stages of starting your company, you'll be figuring out cash flow and trying to get a handle on the books. Grow as fast as is sustainable so you don't have to hire and lay people off, since job security is key to feeling safe. Remember that, in the same way your customers look for the customer promise every time they interact with you, your team members need consistency and reliability as well. Your employees require a consistent experience every day they come to work. If one day they are praised and the next day berated, the inconsistency will have a damaging effect on them. Employees are looking for a friendly environment where they are free to ask questions, make mistakes, and try something that's never been done before.

Safety starts with you; how you treat your direct team members will filter down to how they treat everyone else. If you have a hard time dealing with the stress of starting a business, find an outlet, call a mentor or coach, step out of the office for a minute, but don't misdirect the fear and frustration at others. There is no faster way for a company to crumble than to have a leader give into fear or anger and have that be misdirected at their employees. I wish I could say I've always been perfect at this, but the truth is I haven't. I've let fear in the shape of imposter syndrome overcome my better judgement at times, and it has affected the business. An easy way to get recentered and provide safety is in the next section.

Gratitude/Respect

No one has to climb the mountain with you; every person in your organization is doing it willingly. Every one of them. Yes, you are paying them, and yes, you did buy the foosball table. But in the end, it comes down to the fact that no one has to join your adventure. Because of this, there's a lot to be grateful for: these amazing people chose to be on your team and to help you make it to the summit. And the truth is, summiting requires a good deal of help. In the case of Kilimanjaro, we needed many hands to carry the food for five days and to help with the gear and safety equipment. Neither you, nor even Shackleton, could do it alone. It can be easy to put people into an organizational chart and see them as cogs in a machine; but every one of these amazing people are humans with hopes, dreams, and families just like you.

Take the time, every day, to express appreciation for someone in your organization. Sincerely thank them for coming on the journey with you. And when someone has a victory, celebrate—buy a large gong for the office to strike when someone lands a big deal or finishes a big project. Then take the time to get to know them, their families, and find out what they like to do on the weekends or when they're not at the office. Express a sincere interest in getting to know your employees on a personal level and that culture will proliferate throughout your organization.

Growth

Along with a desire to contribute, people love to grow and become more. It's part of our DNA and the natural cycle of life. And being part of a fast-growing company is a great way to build morale. Providing ways for team members to grow within an organization and personally develop is also a great way to build a positive culture. Start with ways your team members can enhance their skills in their particular area of focus. Invest in personal development programs and sometimes mix it up and have a fun date night where they learn to paint or cook a fancy meal.

You may be at the stage of your business where it is just you and one or two employees, or where you're hitting key growth milestones and are hiring multiple teams of people. If it is just a few of you, it's easy to create your culture and build on these principles. As you grow, it becomes harder to maintain, however, and the buzz and excitement that runs through the halls of your company may begin to diminish. If you have these tenets of culture baked in from the beginning, it will be far easier than trying to turn your corporate version of a cruise liner already at sea. As companies grow, there will naturally be more levels in the organization. The best way to continue to have an amazing culture is to set out the guidelines at the top and then pass them down so that each level of the company is enabled to enact these principles. Empower every director and have them empower each manager with the same.

Communication

A positive culture is one with open lines of communication. Have a way that everyone is proactively heard and emphasize the ideas rather than who is suggesting them. Let go of ego, imposter syndrome, status, or any other limiting factor and realize you can learn something from everyone you meet. Sometimes the most unassuming person will have the most brilliant solution.

In my media agency, a young college student named Tyler walked in the door and said he wanted to work as an intern…for free. I hired him on the spot. I had him apprentice with my lead developer on a mission-critical project—the most important project we had ever done to this point. It even developed into my second business: a digital sheet music company. The developer worked with Tyler under his wing for several months but kept bumping into critical issues. One day he came into my office, threw his hands in the air, and exclaimed that the whole thing was impossible. This was devastating news because of the significance of the project and the amount of investment we had put into it. We talked through things and he convinced me the way the project was architected made it impossible to complete.

After returning from a weekend of much thought, I was greeted by a smiling Tyler. He asked, "Can I show you something?" He went on to demo a working prototype of the entire project! He had architected a different version when he first started working for us and had been developing it at night and on weekends for months. The lead developer had mentored Tyler well, and the project didn't even skip a beat (pun intended). Never underestimate someone's feedback or potential because they are new, young, old, or anything in between.

Overcoming Pitfall 16: Nurture Culture

- Make a list of your employees and quiz yourself on the names of their spouses or significant others. Can you name their children as well? If not, spend some time with them and get to know them better.

- Write out what you hope the culture is inside your company until the goal is reached. Make a plan and start enacting it today.

- Every quarter, identify and work on one trait you can change within yourself as the leader to build a culture you would want to work in.

- Buy a box of 250 blank note cards and envelopes and write one sincere hand-written thank-you letter every workday.

- Create regular activities that humanize and connect everyone at the office. Go running together, have regular foosball tournaments, get off thirty minutes early on Wednesday and play pickleball or racquetball together, have a regular music night or any other activity native to your company.

- Make sure the communication lines are open and everyone feels comfortable giving feedback. Pick three random team members and ask if they feel heard.

- Need ideas about building culture? Go to the website for specific ideas on how you can build culture. EntrepreneursParadox.com/Culture

Conclusion

I started this book at Giordano's Deep Dish Pizzeria in Chicago, as my friend Greg and I reflected on the mountains we've climbed along our individual entrepreneurial journeys. I've come to learn that everyone's story is unique, but the pitfalls remain remarkably the same.

Climbing the entrepreneurial mountain is hard. Intensely hard. It is also wondrous, adventurous, exciting, enriching, enlivening, momentous, and memorable. Every detail permanently etched into memory. There is no one better positioned to lead your expedition up the mountain than you. Step out of the swamp where a majority of entrepreneurs get stuck and see the mountain calling you from above. Doing so can cast you as the hero in your story and provide an adventure worthy of your own book.

The journey up the mountain will require you to grow in ways you never imagined. You will have to leave the old behind and come to life as someone who is the leader of the expedition. As you gain new heights, you will start to view things in new and exciting ways. You will find a purpose and passion similar to the passion you had when you developed your original product or offered your first service to another.

Don't rise up the mountain alone. Climb with mentors, peers, and friends. Most of all, enjoy the journey and sing as you go. Even though the summit is glorious, the trail is where the transformation will happen. Don't wait for the reward at the top to find joy and contentment, find joy every step of the way among your fellow travelers and with the realization that you are growing and becoming. Find the best way up the mountain for you, and remember the most

efficient way to the summit so you can do it over and over again.
When you get to the top, celebrate and do it in grand fashion. Let the
joy of a job well done be commemorated.

The paradox, of course, is that the skills and passions that prompted
you to strike out and build something of your own are the very things
standing in your way. And while you cannot go up the mountain
without coming down changed, becoming a successful entrepreneur
will force you to change at the onset. That's not an easy ask, and
why so few are equipped to do so. Change you must and change you
will: at the mountain's base, at the various camps along the way, and
when you plant your flag on the summit. As the poet Tuli Kupferberg
penned, "When patterns are broken, new worlds emerge."

There's nothing like standing atop your own mountain and seeing
the majesty of a new world beneath. And once you've made it, the
journey isn't over—it's time to turn around and lift others. Find those
you can be a guide to and help them reach their potential and make it
to the top of their own mountain.

THE END

References

Anderson, M. (Writer). (1946). *Joan of Lorraine.*

Armstrong, G. (2018, December 26). How Exercise Affects Your Brain. Retrieved September 11, 2020, from www.scientificamerican.com/article/how-exercise-affects-your-brain/

Arnette, A. (2020, May 23). A New Route on Everest this Spring? Retrieved August 19, 2020, from www.rei.com/blog/climb/a-new-route-on-everest-this-spring.

CDC—Drowsy Driving—Sleep and Sleep Disorders. (2017, March 21). Retrieved September 12, 2020, from www.cdc.gov/sleep/about_sleep/drowsy_driving.html.

Chen, J. (2020, August 28). Unicorn Definition. Retrieved September 09, 2020, from www.investopedia.com/terms/u/unicorn.asp.

Chen, J. (2020, August 29). Private Equity Definition. Retrieved September 09, 2020, from www.investopedia.com/terms/p/privateequity.asp.

Chen, J. (2020, May 25). Nasdaq. Retrieved September 08, 2020, from www.investopedia.com/terms/n/nasdaq.asp.

Chen, J. (2020, September 16). What is a Blue Chip? Retrieved September 18, 2020, from www.investopedia.com/terms/b/bluechip.asp.

Crenshaw, D. (2010, August 20). Is multi-tasking a myth? Retrieved August 24, 2020, from www.bbc.com/news/magazine-11035055.

Culture. (n.d.). Retrieved September 12, 2020, from www.merriam-webster.com/dictionary/culture.

Customer Acquisition Cost: The One Metric That Can Determine Your Company's Fate. (2020, January 24). Retrieved September 12, 2020, from neilpatel.com/blog/customer-acquisition-cost/

Customer Lifetime Value (CLV or LTV). (n.d.). Retrieved September 18, 2020, from www.klipfolio.com/resources/kpi-examples/saas-metrics/customer-lifetime-value.

Definition of Cash Runway. (n.d.). Retrieved September 12, 2020, from www.davemanuel.com/investor-dictionary/cash-runway/

Early to bed, early to rise? (n.d.). Retrieved September 12, 2020, from
    www.utoronto.ca/news/early-bed-early-rise.

FeaturedPsychology·August 22, 2., FeaturedNeurologyPainPsychology·August
    22, 2., FeaturedOpen Neuroscience ArticlesPsychology·August 21, 2.,
    FeaturedNeuroscience·April 28, 2., Also, S., & FeaturedGeneticsNeurology·August
    12, 2. (2017, April 28). Multitasking Overloads the Brain. Retrieved August 24,
    2020, from neurosciencenews.com/multitasking-brain-overload-6531/

Feigenbaum, E. (2017, November 21). Definition of Business Trends. Retrieved
    September 12, 2020, from smallbusiness.chron.com/definition-business-
    trends-3399.html.

Group, R. (n.d.). Center for Sales Research: RAIN Group. Retrieved September 12,
    2020, from www.rainsalestraining.com/sales-research.

Gunjahalli, R. (2020, March 13). Five Reasons Why Every Entrepreneur Needs A Great
    Mentor. Retrieved September 09, 2020, from
    www.entrepreneur.com/article/347638.

Habit 2: Begin with End in Mind. (n.d.). Retrieved September 07, 2020, from
    www.franklincovey.com/the-7-habits/habit-2.html.

Hall, M. (2020, August 28). Who or What Is Dow Jones? Retrieved September 08, 2020,
    from www.investopedia.com/ask/answers/who-or-what-is-dow-jones/

Hayes, A. (2020, August 17). Inside the Average Annual Growth Rate (AAGR).
    Retrieved September 08, 2020, from www.investopedia.com/terms/a/aagr.asp.

Imposter Syndrome in the Workplace. (2018, June 26). Retrieved September 09, 2020,
    from www.leadmd.com/best-practices/blog/imposter-syndrome-in-workplace/

Kagan, J. (2020, September 07). Fiduciary. Retrieved September 12, 2020, from
    www.investopedia.com/terms/f/fiduciary.asp.

Kenton, W. (2020, August 28). S&P 500 Index. Retrieved September 08, 2020, from
    www.investopedia.com/terms/s/sp500.asp.

Kenton, W. (2020, January 29). Understanding the Burn Rate. Retrieved September 12,
    2020, from www.investopedia.com/terms/b/burnrate.asp.

Klucken, T., Tabbert, K., Schweckendiek, J., Merz, C. J., Kagerer, S., Vaitl, D., & Stark,
    R. (2009). Contingency learning in human fear conditioning involves the ventral
    striatum. *Human Brain Mapping, 30*(11), 3636-3644. doi:10.1002/hbm.20791.

Majaski, C. (2020, August 09). Definition of Year-Over-Year (YOY). Retrieved
    September 08, 2020, from www.investopedia.com/terms/y/year-over-year.asp.

Mautz, S. (2017, May 11). Psychology and Neuroscience Blow-Up the Myth of Effective
    Multitasking. Retrieved August 24, 2020, from www.inc.com/scott-mautz/
    psychology-and-neuroscience-blow-up-the-myth-of-effective-multitasking.html.

Medina, J. (2014). *Brain rules: 12 principles for surviving and thriving at work, home,
    and school*. Seattle, WA: Pear Press.

Nov 12, 2. (n.d.). The Average Age of Successful Entrepreneurs Is Actually 45.
    Retrieved September 14, 2020, from knowledge.wharton.upenn.edu/article/age-
    of-successful-entrepreneurs/.

Pinker, S. (2018, October 25). When It Comes to Sleep, One Size Fits All. Retrieved
    September 12, 2020, from www.wsj.com/articles/when-it-comes-to-sleep-one-
    size-fits-all-1540481975.

Predictable Fear. (2014, October 31). Retrieved September 22, 2020, from
    www.psychologytoday.com/us/blog/prefrontal-nudity/201410/predictable-fear.

Rampton, J. (2015, May 21). How a Mentor Can Increase the Success of Your Business.
    Retrieved September 09, 2020, from www.inc.com/john-rampton/how-a-mentor-
    can-increase-the-success-of-your-business.html.

Randler, C. (2009, December 09). Proactive People Are Morning People1. Retrieved
    September 12, 2020, from onlinelibrary.wiley.com/doi/abs/10.1111/j.1559-
    1816.2009.00549.x.

Schultz, M. (2016, February 16). Average Sales Win Rates: How Do You Compare?
    Retrieved September 12, 2020, from www.rainsalestraining.com/blog/average-
    sales-win-rates-how-do-you-compare.

Speech by SEC Commissioner: Diversity in the Boardroom Yields Dividends. (2009,
    September 10). Retrieved September 12, 2020, from www.sec.gov/news/
    speech/2009/spch091009laa.htm.

Staff, M. (2018, January 19). What Is an IPO? Retrieved September 07, 2020, from
    www.fool.com/knowledge-center/what-is-an-ipo-2.aspx.

Taylor, J. (2011, March 30). Technology: Myth of Multitasking. Retrieved August
    24, 2020, from www.psychologytoday.com/us/blog/the-power-prime/201103/
    technology-myth-multitasking.

The True Cost of Multi-Tasking. (2012, September 18). Retrieved August 24, 2020, from www.psychologytoday.com/us/blog/brain-wise/201209/the-true-cost-multi-tasking.

Tuovila, A. (2020, June 29). Cash Flow. Retrieved September 12, 2020, from www.investopedia.com/terms/c/cashflow.asp.

Vidal, R. (2017, April 20). Multitasking Doesn't Work. Retrieved August 24, 2020, from www.huffpost.com/entry/multitasking-doesnt-work_b_9721508.

Resources

www.EntrepreneursParadox.com/ActivityTracker

A printable version of the Wrestling Alligators worksheet.

www.EntrepreneursParadox.com/MountainSurvey

Find out which mountain is best for you.

www.EntrepreneursParadox.com/CaseStudies

Read more case studies on the different business types.

www.EntrepreneursParadox.com/AccurateGoal

Register your goal on the website for additional accountability and reporting.

www.EntrepreneursParadox.com/CalculateGrowthRate

Calculate your desired growth rate for your company.

www.EntrepreneursParadox.com/CompareGrowthRates

Compare your growth rate to get the most up-to-date stats
for growth rates of other companies in your industry.

www.EntrepreneursParadox.com/GoalInfographic

Enter your data to get a visual representation of your goal as an infographic.

www.EntrepreneursParadox.com/FearAssessment

Take the fear assessment.

www.EntrepreneursParadox.com/FearSmashing

Print a version of the five steps worksheet to overcoming fear.

www.EntrepreneursParadox.com/ImposterSyndrome

Discover which of the seven types of imposter syndrome you relate to most.

www.EntrepreneursParadox.com/Hats

Do a search for accountants in your area.

www.EntrepreneursParadox.com/Apps

Find the most up-to-date business apps.

www.EntrepreneursParadox.com/Network

Find an entrepreneur support group in your area.

www.EntrepreneursParadox.com/LeaderSurvey

Take the leader assessment.

www.EntrepreneursParadox.com/PowerHour

Create your own Power Hour using the schedule builder tool.

www.EntrepreneursParadox.com/PeacePlan

Create a Peace Plan.

www.EntrepreneursParadox.com/ProtectTheAsset

Find additional articles and resources on Protecting the Asset.

www.EntrepreneursParadox.com/CAC

Find your industry-specific CAC/CLTV ratio.

www.EntrepreneursParadox.com/Dashboard

See examples of other dashboards and upload yours to help other entrepreneurs.

www.EntrepreneursParadox.com/Formulas

Access a spreadsheet with all the Business Acumen formulas.

www.EntrepreneursParadox.com/Acumen

Request a free Business Acumen consultation.

www.EntrepreneursParadox.com/MarketingPlan

Find example marketing plans.

www.EntrepreneursParadox.com/SalesStrategy

Find an example of a sales strategy

www.EntrepreneursParadox.com/Excited

Share your excitement statements with other entrepreneurs.

www.EntrepreneursParadox.com/Entity

Use the business entity calculator.

www.EntrepreneursParadox.com/OA

www.EntrepreneursParadox.com/Culture

www.EntrepreneursParadox.com/ToDo

www.EntrepreneursParadox.com/Notebook

About the Author

Curtis J. Morley is a serial entrepreneur, educator, speaker, thought leader, patent holder, innovator, businessman, and coach. He is the founder and CEO of The Entrepreneur's Paradox and the director of the Kahlert Initiative on Technology at the University of Utah.

Curtis was formerly the president and Chief Growth Officer of eLearning Brothers (eLB), one of the fastest-growing companies in Utah for six straight years. Throughout this tenure, he helped the company achieve tenfold growth in five years, acquiring 96 of the Fortune 100 as clients, and becoming the third largest brand in eLearning.

Prior to eLearning Brothers, Curtis founded several successful multimillion-dollar companies that include one of the world's premier award-winning interactive agencies, the world's first interactive digital sheet music company, and an entrepreneur coaching company to help bring startup founders to the next level in their businesses. In between his entrepreneurial ventures, Curtis also served as head of Corporate and Global Marketing for FranklinCovey.

Curtis is a sought-after speaker and has done keynotes and speaking engagements around the globe in places such as the UK, China, Japan, New Zealand, and Portugal, including Adobe Max, GCCCE (Global Chinese Conference for Computing in Education), CLOXchange, and E-learning Dev Con.

Curtis has been honored with many awards and recognitions including the Reed Smoot Entrepreneur of the Year, Utah Business Magazine's and Utah Valley Magazine's 40 under 40, Big Business and Technology Award—Best Technology, among others. Curtis sits on several boards and advisory committees of corporations, universities, and nonprofit foundations.

Curtis has also been recognized as:

- Inc. 500 Sixth Fastest-Growing Education Company in US
- Inc. 500/5000 Hall of Fame recipient
- International Company of the Year
- Mountain West Capital Fastest Growing Company
- Peak 100 Companies
- Hot 100 Entrepreneurs
- Brandon Hall Gold, Silver, Bronze
- Tech 10—People's Choice, Experts Choice, Best Sales Traction
- Fab 40

Curtis has five children who he loves dearly. Outside of business, Curtis loves to compete in marathons, Ironman triathlons, and two-hundred-mile relay races. He has a passion for music—singing, playing guitar, and songwriting. One of his favorite things is to sit on his deck on a hot summer night playing in sync with the chorus of crickets in his backyard in the foothills of Utah.

www.EntrepreneursParadox.com

About Entrepreneur's Paradox

Curtis Morley started The Entrepreneur's Paradox with a goal of helping one million entrepreneurs find next-level success. Curtis has an uncanny way of changing the trajectory of a business in a short amount of time. Did you find value in the principles of this book and want to take things to the next level?

Find out how to change your business at www.EntrepreneursParadox.com.

Schedule Curtis to Speak at Your Event

Are you planning an event for your organization? Schedule Curtis to deliver an engaging keynote or work session tailored to your leaders or audience.

- Association and Industry Conferences
- Sales Conferences
- Annual Meetings
- Leadership Development
- Executive and Board Retreats
- Company Functions
- Onsite Consulting
- Client Engagements

Curtis is a sought-after speaker and has presented keynotes and speaking engagements around the globe in places such as the USA, UK, China, Japan, New Zealand, and Portugal.

To schedule Curtis today, email speaking@EntrepreneursParadox.com or go to www.EntrepreneursParadox.com/Speaking.

Suggested Reading List for Entrepreneurs

The Trust Edge: How Top Leaders Gain Faster Results, Deeper Relationships, and a Stronger Bottom Line
   —David Horsager
   David Horsager reveals the foundation of genuine success—trust. Based on research, *The Trust Edge* shows trust is quantifiable and brings dramatic results to businesses and leaders. Horsager teaches readers how to build the Eight Pillars of Trust.

The 4 Disciplines of Execution: Achieving Your Wildly Important Goals
   —Chris McChesney, Sean Covey, Jim Huling
   The 4 Disciplines of Execution (4DX) is a simple, repeatable, and proven formula for executing your most important strategic priorities in the midst of the whirlwind.

Good to Great: Why Some Companies Make the Leap and Others Don't
   —Jim Collins
   Start with 1,435 good companies. Examine their performance over forty years. Find the eleven companies that became great. Now here's how you can do it too. Lessons on eggs, flywheels, hedgehogs, buses, and other essentials of business that can help you transform your company.

Management Mess to Leadership Success: 30 Challenges to Become the Leader You Would Follow
   —Scott Jeffrey Miller
   In Miller's *Management Mess to Leadership Success*, you'll find thirty leadership challenges that can, when applied, change the way you manage yourself, lead others, and produce results. The wisdom in Scott's book was learned through hard knocks and was honed by Stephen R. Covey and the FranklinCovey team through years of research and corporate training experience.

The Myth of Multitasking: How "Doing It All" Gets Nothing Done
   —Dave Crenshaw
   In a compelling business fable, *The Myth of Multitasking* confronts a popular idea
   that has come to define our hectic, work-a-day world. This simple yet powerful
   book shows clearly why multitasking is, in fact, a lie that wastes time and costs
   money. Far from being efficient, multitasking actually damages productivity and
   relationships at work and at home.

The 7 Habits of Highly Successful People: Powerful Lessons in Personal Change
   —Stephen R. Covey
   In *The 7 Habits of Highly Effective People*, author Stephen R. Covey presents
   a holistic, integrated, principle-centered approach for solving personal and
   professional problems. With penetrating insights and pointed anecdotes, Covey
   reveals a step-by-step pathway for living with fairness, integrity, service, and
   human dignity—principles that give us the security to adapt to change and the
   wisdom and power to take advantage of the opportunities that change creates.

Essentialism: The Disciplined Pursuit of Less
   —Greg McKeown
   Essentialism is more than a time-management strategy or a productivity
   technique. It is a systematic discipline for discerning what is absolutely essential,
   then eliminating everything that is not, so we can make the highest possible
   contribution toward the things that really matter.

The 5 Choices: The Path to Extraordinary Productivity
   —Kory Kogon, Adam Merril, Leena Rinne
   From the business experts at FranklinCovey, *The 5 Choices* is an exploration
   of modern productivity. It offers powerful insights drawn from the latest
   neuroscience research and decades of experience in the time-management field to
   help you master your attention and energy management.

The Power of Habit: Why We Do What We Do in Life and Business
   —Charles Duhigg
   In *The Power of Habit*, award-winning business reporter Charles Duhigg takes us
   to the thrilling edge of scientific discoveries that explain why habits exist and how
   they can be changed.

The Speed of Trust: The One Thing That Changes Everything
   —Stephen M. R. Covey
   The Speed of Trust offers an unprecedented and eminently practical look at

exactly how trust functions in every transaction and every relationship—from the most personal to the broadest, most indirect interaction.

StrengthsFinder 2.0
—From Gallup
In its latest national bestseller, *StrengthsFinder 2.0*, Gallup unveils the new and improved version of its popular assessment, language of thirty-four themes, and much more (see below for details). While you can read this book in one sitting, you'll use it as a reference for decades.

The 4 Hour Workweek: Escape 9–5, Live Anywhere, and Join the New Rich
—Timothy Ferris
Forget the old concept of retirement and the rest of the deferred-life plan—there is no need to wait and every reason not to, especially in unpredictable economic times. Whether your dream is escaping the rat race, experiencing high-end world travel, or earning a monthly five-figure income with zero management, *The 4-Hour Workweek* is the blueprint.

Venture Deals: Be Smarter Than Your Lawyer and Venture Capitalist
—Brad Feld
The new edition of *Venture Deals* continues to show fledgling entrepreneurs the inner workings of the VC process, from the venture capital term sheet and effective negotiating strategies to the initial seed and the later stages of development.

Crucial Conversations: Tools for Talking When Stakes Are High
—Kerry Patterson
Crucial Conversations gives you the tools you need to step up to life's most difficult and important conversations, say what's on your mind, and achieve the positive resolutions you want.

Leadership and Self Deception: Getting Out of the Box
—The Arbinger Institute
Through a story everyone can relate to about a man facing challenges on the job and in his family, the authors expose the fascinating ways that we can blind ourselves to our true motivations and unwittingly sabotage the effectiveness of our own efforts to achieve success and increase happiness.

Dare to Lead: Brave Work. Tough Conversations. Whole Hearts.
—Brené Brown
Brené Brown has taught us what it means to dare greatly, rise strong, and brave

the wilderness. Now, based on new research conducted with leaders, change makers, and culture shifters, she's showing us how to put those ideas into practice so we can step up and lead.

Seeing the Big Picture: Business Acumen to Build Your Credibility, Career, and Company
    —Kevin Cope
An MBA in under 180 pages, *Seeing the Big Picture* simplifies the complexities of businesses large and small and shows you how a deep understanding of your company can help build the credibility and career you want. And it can make your work more fulfilling and purpose-driven by highlighting how you influence the success of your team, department, or organization.

Multipliers: How the Best Leaders Make Everyone Smarter
    —Liz Wiseman
A thought-provoking, accessible, and essential exploration of why some leaders ("Diminishers") drain capability and intelligence from their teams, while others ("Multipliers") amplify it to produce better results.

Be Brilliant! How to Master the Sales Skill of Persuasive Questioning
    —Scott O. Baird, PhD
Be Brilliant! teaches you how to master the sales skill of persuasive questioning. If you want to be exceptional in the world of sales, *Be Brilliant!* is required reading. Dr. Baird shares some of his greatest insights, breaking down how and when to ask the right questions to increase conversions and maximize your success. Sales leaders and salespeople alike will find enormous value in *Be Brilliant!*

Atomic Habits: An Easy & Proven Way to Build Good Habits & Break Bad Ones
    —James Clear
No matter your goals, *Atomic Habits* offers a proven framework for improving— every day. James Clear, one of the world's leading experts on habit formation, reveals practical strategies that will teach you exactly how to form good habits, break bad ones, and master the tiny behaviors that lead to remarkable results.

Extreme Ownership: How US Navy SEALs Lead and Win
    —Jocko Willink and Leif Babin
Two US Navy SEAL officers who led the most highly decorated special operations unit of the Iraq War demonstrate how to apply powerful leadership principles from the battlefield to business and life.

The Book of Joy: Lasting Happiness in a Changing World
—His Holiness the Dalai Lama and Archbishop Desmond Tutu
Nobel Peace Prize Laureates His Holiness the Dalai Lama and Archbishop
Desmond Tutu have survived more than fifty years of exile and the soul-crushing
violence of oppression. Despite their hardships—or, as they would say, because of
them—they are two of the most joyful people on the planet.

Start with Why: How Great Leaders Inspire Everyone to Take Action
—Simon Sinek
Start with Why shows that the leaders who've had the greatest influence in the
world all think, act, and communicate the same way—and it's the opposite of
what everyone else does. Sinek calls this powerful idea The Golden Circle, and it
provides a framework upon which organizations can be built, movements can be
led, and people can be inspired. And it all starts with *why*.

Made to Stick: Why Some Ideas Survive and Others Die
—Chip and Dan Heath
In *Made to Stick*, Chip and Dan Heath reveal the anatomy of ideas that stick and
explain ways to make ideas stickier, such as applying the human scale principle,
using the Velcro Theory of Memory, and creating curiosity gaps. Along the way,
we discover that sticky messages of all kinds—from the infamous "kidney theft
ring" hoax to a coach's lessons on sportsmanship to a vision for a new product at
Sony—draw their power from the same six traits.

FIU Business Press equips professionals with the essential tools and skills for business success in a rapidly evolving world. An imprint of Mango Publishing, FIU Business Press is part of Florida International University's College of Business, a top-ranked school by *U.S. News & World Report*. The college has been recognized as the nation's #2 international business program, #8 international MBA, and #22 online master's in business. Based in Miami, FIU has been named a top-50 innovative public university and is the nation's fourth largest university with a student body of more than 54,000.

Mango Publishing, which publishes an eclectic list of books by diverse authors, was named 2019 and 2020's #1 fastest growing independent publisher by *Publishers Weekly*. Through a partnership of FIU College of Business office of Executive Education and Mango Publishing, FIU Business Press shares innovative, yet practical, business knowledge that allows professionals and executives to thrive globally.

Help us fuel business growth by sharing your thoughts and ideas:

Read about FIU's business programs:
business.fiu.edu/executive-education

Email us: FiuExecEd@fiu.edu

Follow us on LinkedIn:
Florida International University- College of Business
FIU Executive Education

Newsletter: mangopublishinggroup.com/newsletter